Science and Technology in Society

D0061486

Key Themes in Sociology

This outstanding introductory series covers major theoretical perspectives and key concepts reflecting contemporary society. Written in an engaging style and accessible format, these concise volumes are designed to stimulate student discussion and thought. Pedagogical features such as primary readings, chapter summaries, key terms, and further suggested reading ensure these student-friendly volumes will be an essential aid to the study of the key themes in sociology.

Gender Theory and Research: An Introduction
Amy S. Wharton

Science and Technology in Society: From Biotechnology to the Internet
Daniel Lee Kleinman

Forthcoming:

Citizenship
Peter Kivisto and Thomas Faist

Science and Technology in Society

From Biotechnology to the Internet

Daniel Lee Kleinman

Blackwell
Publishing

© 2005 by Daniel Lee Kleinman

BLACKWELL PUBLISHING
350 Main Street, Malden, MA 02148-5020, USA
9600 Garsington Road, Oxford OX4 2DQ, UK
500 Swanston Street, Carlton, Victoria 3053, Australia

The right of Daniel Lee Kleinman to be identified as the Author of this Work has been asserted in accordance with the UK Copyright, Designs, and Patents Act 1988.

All rights reserved. No part of this publication may be reproduced, stored in a retrieval system, or transmitted, in any form or by any means, electronic, mechanical, photocopying, recording or otherwise, except as permitted by the UK Copyright, Designs, and Patents Act 1988, without the prior permission of the publisher.

First published 2005 by Blackwell Publishing Ltd

3   2008

Library of Congress Cataloging-in-Publication Data

Kleinman, Daniel Lee.
  Science and technology in society : from biotechnology to the internet / Daniel Lee Kleinman.
    p. cm. – (Key themes in sociology)
  Includes bibliographical references and index.
  ISBN 978-0-631-23181-3 (hard cover : alk. paper)
  ISBN 978-0-631-23182-0 (pbk. : alk. paper)
1. Science–Social aspects. 2. Technology–Social aspects.
3. Science and civilization. 4. Technology and
civilization. I. Title. II. Series.
  Q175.5.K537 2005
  303.48′3–dc22

                                                          2005007227

A catalogue record for this title is available from the British Library.

Set in 10 on 12 pt Sabon
by SNP Best-set Typesetter Ltd, Hong Kong
Printed and bound in Singapore
by Fabulous Printers Pte Ltd

The publisher's policy is to use permanent paper from mills that operate a sustainable forestry policy, and which has been manufactured from pulp processed using acid-free and elementary chlorine-free practices. Furthermore, the publisher ensures that the text paper and cover board used have met acceptable environmental accreditation standards.

For further information on
Blackwell Publishing, visit our website:
www.blackwellpublishing.com

To Jack,
who turned me to the study of science and technology 20 years ago

and

To Flora and Susan,
who make certain that studying science and technology isn't all I do

Contents

Acknowledgments

This book is a product of a number of years of contemplating and talking about science and technology. In it, I have tried to crystallize my thinking in a way that will be accessible to undergraduate students and general readers. So, the first people I would like to thank are the undergraduate students who have taken my courses at the University of Houston–Clear Lake, Georgia Tech, and the University of Wisconsin. Discussing the kind of matters considered in this book with students over a bit more than a decade has sharpened my thinking, and I hope what I have written here reflects that clarity.

So many colleagues over the years have made considering, discussing, and writing about science and technology a pleasure. I want to thank all of my former colleagues in the School of History, Technology, and Society at Georgia Tech and my current colleagues in the Department of Rural Sociology and the Holtz Center for Science and Technology Studies at the University of Wisconsin–Madison. Both Georgia Tech and Wisconsin have provided nurturing and energizing workplaces.

I have benefited from ongoing discussion with an array of individuals over the years. Among them are: Fred Buttel, Scott Frickel, Jo Handelsman, David Hess, Allen Hunter, Brian Martin, Kelly Moore, and, most recently, Samer Alatout. Their thinking is certainly reflected in this work, as is that of many of my collaborators, including Abby Kinchy, Hans Klein, and Steve Vallas.

My parents – Barbara and Jerry Kleinman – continue to support me on my intellectual journey, and beyond their constant and enriching presence in my life, over many years they have peppered me with news articles, many of which are cited in this book.

Financially, I received support that made this project possible from two sources – the Graduate School at the University of Wisconsin–Madison and two Hatch grants from the United States Department of Agriculture and the State of Wisconsin.

I cannot thank the staff at Blackwell enough for their help and support. The idea for this book emerged from discussions with Susan Rabinowitz, formerly at Blackwell. Without Susan, there wouldn't be a book. Since Susan left the press, Ken Provencher has been my editor. His gentle prodding since I started working on the project has kept the effort moving forward, and I have appreciated his kind encouragement and advice. I have benefited also from the two reviewers of the manuscript – Sandra Harding and an anonymous colleague. Each provided insights that have, I believe, made the book stronger; and happily, Sandra's review provided the basis for solidifying loose links that we developed some years ago.

And finally . . . this book is dedicated to three people. First, to Jack Kloppenburg. Jack has been the single biggest influence on my professional development over the past 20 years. He served as my mentor in graduate school, where I became his collaborator and where we became friends. He has supported me unequivocally during the past two decades, and I couldn't be more pleased that we are now in the same department. My partner, Susan Bernstein, and my daughter, Flora Berklein, are the other people to whom I dedicate this book. Susan and I have swapped ideas, shared a household, and raised a child for a long time now. How lucky I am. Since her birth in 1992, Flora has been a wonderful presence in my life, with every query and every hug making life so worth living.

Abbreviations

AZT	zidovudine (generic name), antiviral drug
Bt	*Bacillus thuringiensis* (soil bacterium)
Cre-*lox*P	recombination system
EPA	US Environmental Protection Agency
FDA	US Food and Drug Administration
GM	genetically modified
GMC	genetically modified crops
GMO	genetically modified organisms
HRC	herbicide resistant crops
rBGH	recombinant Bovine Growth Hormone
rBST	recombinant Bovine Somatotropin (= rBGH)
rDNA	recombinant DNA
S&E	science and engineering
Taq	polymerase used in amplification of DNA
USDA	US Department of Agriculture

1

Science is Political/Technology is Social: Concerns, Concepts, and Questions

As the twenty-first century dawns, science and technology are central features of the lives of people worldwide. Whether it is the medical tests received by a loved one, the threats to one's job posed by mechanization or computerization, the chemical factory in one's neighborhood, or policies about global warming, in ways large and small science and technology affect our lives. This is as true if we live in Ames, Iowa as in Bhopal, India. Technoscience is a feature of our lives, whether we work in the dairy industry in Vermont, the computer industry in Japan, or the apparel industry in Korea. Certainly, depending on our location we will be affected in different ways, but we will be affected all the same.

Citizenship in this technoscientific world demands that we learn to grasp the issues raised by our environment. We must nurture the building of tools that will allow us to engage in a critical understanding of developments in science and technology. The aim of this book is to provide a set of such tools – critical concepts for the assessment of science and technology. In doing so, I do not mean to imply that these are the only concepts that can be used to analytically engage the world of science and technology. They are one lens through which to study, analyze, and evaluate the practices and products of technoscience. The concepts I elaborate have been useful for me. I believe they are cogent and compelling. Some readers may feel the same. But this book will count as a success if the arguments I present in the pages to follow prompt readers to think about science and technology differently, whether or not they agree with my approach.

To say that this book is about the provision of tools for looking at science and technology is somewhat misleading. In fact, in only one part of this chapter do I actually explicitly lay out the kinds of orienting concepts that I use in thinking about technoscience. This is preceded by a discussion of why it is so difficult for many people – especially Americans – to think critically about science and technology.

The remainder of the book uses these concepts in discussions of several distinct cases that deal with matters of science and technology. In chapter 2 ("Ceding Debate: Biotechnology and Agriculture"), I consider how recent developments in biotechnology are affecting the social organization of agriculture. Here, I pay special attention to farming and the relationship between farming and agribusiness. Among the specific technologies I consider are: herbicide resistant crops, the so-called "terminator technology," recombinant bovine growth hormone/bovine somatropin, and the genetically engineered use of *Bacillus thuringiensis*. In addition, I explore the way in which the public controversy over agricultural biotechnology has been framed by the proponents and opponents of the technology.

In chapter 3 ("Rethinking Information Technology: Caught in a World Wide Web"), I stress that to understand the possibilities for computers and the internet we must be attentive to the world into which they enter. My discussion has three parts. First, I consider the so-called digital divide in computer and internet access. Here, I analyze the ways in which computer and information access are stratified across different social groups and regions. Next, I investigate the use of information technologies in educational settings, and finally, I consider what information technology means and is likely to mean for politics and civic life.

Chapter 4 is entitled "Owning Technoscience: Understanding the New Intellectual Property Battles." Intellectual property considerations are central to debates about developments in technoscience. Scientists, business people, and government officials disagree over who should own the human genome, and college students and record executives argue about the free circulation of music on the World Wide Web. How necessary is intellectual property protection to the promotion of innovation and economic growth? Who benefits from patents and copyrights and who is harmed? In this chapter, I interrogate our social common sense about the virtues of intellectual property protection. The chapter suggests the evidence in support of its importance is questionable and that in some instances intellectual property protection may hinder innovation and economic growth. In the second half of the chapter, I discuss the issues of innovation promotion, equity, and social stratification raised by several recent technoscientific developments. This portion of the chapter deals first with digital technologies and later with developments in biology.

Chapter 5 ("Technoscience in the Third World: The Politics of Indigenous Resources") has three sections. First, I investigate the relationship between colonialism and genetic resources, paying special attention to the centrality of these resources in the development of the economic infrastructures of colonial powers and the ways divergent views of knowledge and property are woven through colonial history. Next, I consider how colonial history laid the foundations for current international relations and practices around biological resources. Finally, I provide a discussion of three recent instances where some effort was made to correct historical inequities in north–south relations around biological resources.

In chapter 6 ("Gender and the Ideology of Merit: Women, Men, Science, and Engineering"), I explore the divergent experiences of men and women in science and engineering training and careers. I begin by critiquing the idea that the world of science is meritocratic. I contend that technoscience is a fundamentally social institution and that the experiences of men and women in it are shaped by its social organization and the larger social world in which science and engineering are embedded. The chapter considers the experiences of men and women both in academia and science-based industry.

Finally, in chapter 7 ("Democracy and Expertise: Citizenship in the High-Tech Age"), I consider the roles of lay citizens and experts in a world infused by technoscience. I draw on several case studies to illustrate the often partial character of experts' knowledge on matters of crucial importance to specific communities. Using these cases and several others I also show how the knowledge of people who are not certified experts can improve the quality of understanding on some highly technical matters. In addition, I consider several instances that suggest that arguments of lay incompetence are not valid justifications for excluding non-experts from technical decision-making in areas that affect their lives. Finally, I point to what I believe are the most important barriers to lay understanding in what are traditionally considered expert realms, and suggest ways in which these barriers might be surmounted.

WHY IS THINKING ABOUT SCIENCE AND TECHNOLOGY SO HARD?

I believe two features of our discursive landscape – the realm of ideas, concepts, categories, and the many beliefs we take for granted – make it difficult to think critically about science and technology. I call these discourses *scientism* and *technological progressivism*.[1] Scientism has and long a varied history. Roughly speaking it is the notion that there is an inherent divide between facts and values – that they are intrinsically different categories of phenomena. This idea can be seen in Plato's claim that contemplative thought and practical action should be separated, in the efforts of seventeenth-century European natural philosophers to protect their work from attacks by the church and the state, and in early twentieth-century debates in Germany over values in social science (Proctor 1991). The study of science, according to this way of thinking, demands bracketing values and studying only facts. So not only are facts and values distinct, facts are superior to values in terms of credibility and cognitive authority. This belief in the cognitive superiority of facts over values leads to the conclusion that only trained scientists – *experts at unearthing facts* – can appropriately participate in decision-making on technical matters, where data (the facts) is the product of the scientific method (Kleinman & Kloppenburg 1991).[2]

In this context, the authority of science rests on its claims to be value-free and politically neutral (Nelkin 1995; Proctor 1991). We tend to believe that "the interpretations and predictions of scientists . . . [are] rational and immune from political manipulation because they are based on data gathered through objective procedures" (Nelkin 1995: 452). As a result, we accept that science and scientists are the best possible arbiters of controversy, clearing away the tangle of politics and opinion to reveal the unbiased truth.

Evidence of the unflagging resilience of scientism can be found in controversies over new technology. In many such disputes, those who oppose the technology because of the expected undesirable social effects or moral/ethical concerns gain legitimate entry into the debate only when they focus on issues, such as the environment or health and safety, that are believed to be assessable using recognized scientific methods. A good example of this is the reduction of moral concerns about fetal research into technical debates about the precise point at which life begins (Nelkin 1995: 453). Similarly, US activists opposed to genetically engineered foods have found it strategically effective to focus on their environmental impacts and on worries about food safety and not to openly base their opposition on concerns about, for example, the socioeconomic impacts on small farmers or moral opposition to the commodification of nature. Social impacts and moral concerns are typically considered to be based on value-judgments and are, therefore, viewed as less credible; by contrast, debates about health and safety issues are viewed as adjudicable in scientific terms (cf. Kleinman 1986; Kleinman and Pastor 1989). Thus, such discussions are considered more legitimate.

The second discourse that I believe often inhibits the ability of citizens to view science and especially technology as reasonable subjects for wide-ranging public debate I term *technological progressivism*. This is an idea with roots in the Enlightenment, when progress became a synonym for the good and technology came to be viewed as a tool in all progressive projects (cf. Schatzberg 1999; Smith 1995). Founding leaders of the United States viewed new technologies as a means of realizing the goals of the American revolution (Smith 1995), and by the nineteenth century the equation of technology and progress was firmly established in the American imagination (Noble 1983; Smith 1995; Hard & Jamison 1998; Schatzberg 1999). Thus we have come to take the virtues of technological development for granted and to see technology as self-propelling, moving forward along a singular path without human intervention. In this context, debating technology is generally inappropriate. There are no social choices, as technology has only one path, which is intrinsically determined, and there is no point in blocking the road down which technology proceeds, as it is always for the good.

This view of technology is evident in a wide array of cases. We see it in instances in which certain technologies come to be viewed as progressive, while others are seen as old fashioned. In the development of airplane technology between 1914 and 1945, for example, engineers were captivated by the idea of replacing wooden parts with metal, despite evidence for the virtues of wood, because metal "symbolized progress and science" while wood was viewed as outmoded (Schatzberg 1999: 44). More recently, some analysts have pointed to "technological utopianism" as responsible for pushing computer technology, with relatively little critical examination, into primary and secondary educational settings (Sophia 1998).

If this view drives the development of technology, it is also the basis for dismissing critics of new technologies. Despite the often thoughtful assessment of developing industrial production by nineteenth-century Luddites, the term has taken on a disparaging tone as the twenty-first century begins.[3] In recent years, proponents of biotechnology have attempted to marginalize critics by referring to them as Luddites, alarmists, and champions of technological stagnation. With this kind of overblown rhetoric, one can imagine that there would be little room for careful and deliberate questioning of new technological developments.

TECHNOSCIENCE IS SOCIAL

What does it mean to say that science and technology are social phenomena? The views of science and technology embodied in scientism and technological progressivism leave little room for thinking about technoscience as social. About all we can say is that since science is undertaken by and technology developed by people, and people are social, science and technology are social. But this view of the social character of technoscience is terribly limited. It cannot provide the basis for capturing the complexity of science and technology in the contemporary world. We need a more textured understanding.

The most traditional view of science understands knowledge to be the product of reading reality off of nature. There is nothing between the reader and what is read, and a good reader produces something like truth. From this perspective, the social character of science is not really part of the knowledge production process. Because scientists are human they might, for example, commit fraud, self-consciously misrepresenting their reading of nature, and science could be said to be social in this sense. Adherents to a traditional view would likely also accept that science is social in the sense that who gets to be a scientist may be the result of the social stratification of society at large. Similarly, a traditionalist might view science as social in the sense that what research gets done is determined by what funders – the government, foundations, industry – are willing to support.

These examples are all legitimate cases of the social nature of techno-science. But they construe the social character of science too narrowly. I believe that technoscience is absolutely and thoroughly social. Even the idea that researchers cull truth from nature in an unmediated fashion is mistaken. We never look outside ourselves and see phenomena through entirely naive eyes. How we understand what we see – indeed, for all practical purposes, what we actually see – is shaped by a wide array of prior assumptions, commitments, worldviews, what have you. We are not infinite beings capable of what one analyst calls the godtrick – of seeing everything from nowhere (Haraway 1988). As a consequence, we make selections about where to look, and this affects what we see. By looking to the left instead of the right we end up with a different picture of the world. If we study a prairie, the kinds of *facts* we will *see* will depend on, for example, whether we are looking at a macro level – exploring, for example, the relationship between weather, flora, and fauna – or at a micro level, training our sight on the interactions between bacteria in the soil and the plants growing in the earth. Scientists's training affects where they look, how they look at phenomena they study, and consequently what they see. And, of course, the content of training is thoroughly social. It is developed in educational systems through the interaction of certified scientists. It develops and varies over time and place.

Some philosophers have argued that facts are theory-laden. By that they mean that something we might call "reality" is never seen independent of the theories that allow scientists to think about what they see. In terms used in the philosophy of science, no experience is unmediated (Kuhn 1970; Wing 2000). Theory lies between experience/reality and facts. Scientists are exposed to theories during their training, and again, these shape where scientists look, how they view what they see, and what they see. Consequently, as many analysts have noted, it can happen that unexpected events take place before a scientist's eyes and provoke no response. When no meaning is attached to an experience, the experience may be ignored (Bloor 1976; Angier 1988).

The categories, orientations, and at some level the values on which scientists draw are affected by their disciplinary orientation. Thus, for example, ecologists are likely to look at a biological environment as a system, paying special attention to the interaction of its many components. A geneticist might, instead, be interested in the role that a particular gene plays in the life or fitness of an animal, plant, or microbe.

Or take the case of epidemiology. Epidemiologists study health and disease in populations. The approach used to study this problem is typically modeled on a traditional experimental research design in which, for example, some randomly determined subjects are given a drug and others are given a placebo. Here, other factors that could muddy an assessment of the efficacy of the drug under investigation are held constant or controlled for. In epidemiological research, beyond exposure and non-exposure to the hypothesized disease inducer, other factors are held constant. Where differences in frequency of disease outcome vary by exposure/non-exposure, researchers conclude that the hypothesized inducer causes the disease. But importantly, the orientation of epidemiology does not typically lead analysts to ask questions about "why some individuals but not others were exposed, or what other changes occurred in order to produce the exposures" (Wing 2000: 31). Thus, although epidemiologists identified smoking as a cause of lung cancer, they focused on this as an individual behavior. They did not integrate the role of the tobacco industry, commercial sale of cigarettes, or "the social circumstances that make smoking a rewarding habit" into their analysis (Wing 2000: 37).

There are many other cases that illustrate how disciplinary orientation affects what a scientist sees, but let me just describe one: the case of toxicologists who work on food-safety issues (Busch, Tanaka, & Gunter 2000). These researchers often model their work on the metaphor that "rats are miniature people." This allows toxicologists to study how rats react to suspected food toxins in a controlled experimental setting. They avoid experimenting on humans, which permits them to bypass the practical difficulty of keeping humans in a laboratory setting for months on end to make certain they consume proper quantities of the expected toxin, and they avoid the potential ethical difficulties that might result if human exposure to the suspected toxin led to serious illness. Rats offer other practical advantages: they have a short life-cycle and are relatively inexpensive to maintain. Thus, ethical, temporal, and financial considerations affect the decision to treat rats as people. But this decision is consequential, since rats are not, in fact, people. People and rats are biologically different in ways that could mean that the results of research on rats are not valid for humans.

Beyond disciplines, professional norms can affect the ways in which scientists look at phenomena. In this context, it is helpful to return to the case of epidemiology. Under what conditions do epidemiologists recognize the presence of a carcinogen in an environment they are studying? Scientists talk about two varieties of error: type I and type II. Type I errors amount to false positives. The epidemiologist who makes a type I error might, for example, conclude that a particular environmental contaminant is the cause of a cluster of cancers in a community, when it is not. The researcher who makes a type II error, by contrast, would conclude, in a similar case, that a specific factor is not causing disease, when in fact it is. The issue of values is not far from the surface here. Publishing research containing a type I error could be professionally embarrassing when it is revealed and leads the scientist to retract his or her findings. This could have future impacts on the scientist's career. By contrast, a type II error would lead a scientist to mistakenly miss a discovery, but her or his reputation would not be harmed. Unlike professional epidemiologists, one could imagine that citizens in a community that might have been affected by an environmental carcinogen would have preferred scientists to err on the side of caution and make a type I error, instead of a type II error (Brown & Mikkelsen 1990).

The mediation of experience by theory, worldview, or discipline points to how what scientists see and what they say is affected by social factors. But beyond this, what is accepted as legitimate knowledge is also a product of interpretive practices. One might assume that reproducible experimental results would allow scientists to draw relatively unambiguous conclusions about the piece of nature that is the object of study in the experiment. If this experiment is done following agreed upon methods, should we not imagine that while the social may enter into the equation of how the piece of nature was seen, it stopped there? Perhaps sometimes. However, on other occasions, scientists disagree about how to interpret the results of an experiment or even whether the experiment was properly or competently done. Judgments about these matters are inevitably social. They affect the resolution of controversies in research, and they affect what we take to be knowledge of a phenomenon (Collins 1985; Collins & Pinch 1993; Martin 2005). Harry Collins shows that researchers's ability to replicate a laser technology also depended on informal communication, not solely formal technical rules (Hess 1997: 96). Collins has also provided evidence that a series of negative experiments on gravity waves did not solve a controversy among researchers. Instead, *rhetorical factors* were central in solving the controversy.

Another way we can see science as social is by looking across history at the variation in the definition of science by time and place. If there was something intrinsic or asocial about science, there would be no variation in what counts as science. Instead, what we see is struggles over what should count as science and what should not (see Gieryn 1999). In Victorian England, one leading scientist simultaneously stressed the abstract character of science to distinguish it from mechanics, and the concrete nature of science to distinguish it from religion. Arguing to the religious establishment that science was abstract would have suggested that science might interfere with the theological realm. Suggesting to mechanics that science was concrete would have led mechanics to believe scientists were likely to encroach on their territory.

In the mid-twentieth century, natural and physical scientists differed with social scientists in the United States over whether social science was, indeed, science. In the first skirmish, natural and physical scientists argued that social science was not science, while many social scientists suggested it was. When the issue was revisited a few years later, the position was reversed, with social scientists arguing for difference and natural and physical scientists arguing for similarity (Gieryn 1999). Along similar lines, the definitions of basic and applied science do not reflect the intrinsic character of the work, but are social products (Kloppenburg 1988; Stokes 1997). It is precisely because the line between technology and science is not intrinsic but a social outcome that I often refer to technoscience to avoid making an arbitrary distinction (Latour 1987). In making this point about the social basis and arbitrariness of what counts as science, I do not mean to suggest that absolutely anything could be called science. At the same time, the finite number of characteristics is overwhelmingly large, and the borders of science are "flexibly and discursively mapped out," often "in pursuit of some observed or inferred ambition" (Gieryn 1999: 23).

When we are speaking of artifacts – those things we commonly understand as technologies – their social nature can be seen in many ways. First, the history of technology is replete with cases in which, instead of the one path implied by technological progressivism, there are multiple paths along which a given variety of artifact might proceed or might have proceeded. In other words, there were choices to be made, and there is no evidence that the selection that we came to live with was intrinsically better than the artifact lost to history. The case of airplane-wing technology that I described earlier is one such instance. According to performance criteria, wood might conceivably have been the better choice at the time, but metal symbolized progress – a value held in high regard by involved engineers – and so won out (Schatzberg 1999).

The early history of machine tools – technologies used to make other machines – has similar contours (Noble 1984). It involves choices, and the choices were predicated on values. In the late 1940s, users of machine tools were faced with two types, one called numerical control and the other termed record playback. Numerical control technology was favored by the military because it was more precise than record playback, and the parts the military needed crafted depended on this higher level of precision. On the other hand, numerical control technology was not affordable for small machine shops, and because this technology removed control from the shop floor, workers opposed it. Management in larger firms, however, favored it. In the end, numerical control became the industry standard.

These cases illustrate the social nature of technology by showing that there was a choice to be made and that the criteria for making the choice were not in any reasonable sense technical. These cases also illustrate the fact that technical artifacts embody or are associated with values: valuing progress versus efficacy in one instance, and worker control and small shop affordability versus management control and technical precision in the other instance. There are also cases where artifacts seem to literally embody values. Take, for example, the overpasses that cross Wantagh Parkway to Long Island, New York, and in particular to Jones Beach (Winner 1986). Robert Moses, the designer responsible for these bridges, very consciously decided that they should be built at a height above the parkway that would make it impossible for buses to pass under them. This decision, according to Moses' biographer (Caro 1974), reflected Moses's racial prejudice and social class bias. The low overpasses meant that while more well-to-do whites could use the parkway for commuting and to reach destinations along it for recreation, it would not be accessible for low-income citizens, many of whom were people of color, who needed to rely on public transportation.[4]

TECHNOSCIENCE IS POLITICAL

In my lexicon, to say that a phenomenon is political means that power of some form is implicated. I believe that science and technology are fundamentally and thoroughly political. In fact, it is rather difficult to separate out the social and the political; I have done so for analytical purpose only. In reality, the social and the political are inextricably intertwined. If we see that selection and choice is involved in the practice of science and technology, we must ask why one selection is made over some other. Why is this theory used instead of another one? Why was this technology commercialized and not the other? Surely, nature or reality plays a role here, but as I have shown already, so do values. But showing that values play a role in selection or choice begs the question of why one value instead of another value? The answer, I submit, is power. Power is enabling for actors "on its side" and constraining for actors who oppose it. To say this, I do not mean to suggest that power is an all-or-nothing phenomenon, but that will become clearer in the pages that follow.

Social theory abounds with approaches to power (cf. Marx 1977; Foucault 1972, 1980; Lorber 1994; MacKinnon 1989; Lukes 1974). The way I find most helpful is to think in terms of structures, resources, and discourse. This three-fold distinction is analytical. In the world that humans inhabit – what we sometimes call the social world – the boundary between structures, resources, and discourses is blurry at best. Still, understanding technoscience demands that they be disaggregated. At the most general level, I understand structures to constitute formal and informal, explicit and implicit "rules of play." These entities define specific constraints and opportunities for actors depending on their location in a structural matrix. This matrix might be something as amorphous as the system of class or gender relations or as concrete as a national state or a university laboratory.

What does this mean less abstractly? Let us begin at the most micro level: a university laboratory. Here, there are formal rules that grant certain rights to professors who head them. The laboratory leader is entitled to make decisions about the kind of research that is undertaken, how it is done, and who is responsible for doing the research. The informal cultural authority attributed to the professor who leads the lab – a more diffuse source of power located in the larger society – by students may also make it unlikely that students will challenge the professor's judgment, even when there is no formal prohibition against doing so (Owen-Smith 2001); and, indeed, if this informal cultural authority is sufficiently powerful, the student may never actually consciously contemplate the possibility of posing a challenge. Thus, we can say in this instance that the professor has power over her students.

Looking at a more intermediate level, we might consider national states as structures. Comparing the US state and the states of certain European countries, we can see how structure creates different opportunities and constraints and distributes power differently. The US state is often described as highly fragmented and permeable with multiple points of entry (cf. Kleinman 1995; Skocpol 1985). American political parties are described as undisciplined and non-programmatic. Many European states are seen as considerably less fragmented and permeable, and political parties in many European nations are highly disciplined and programmatic (Lowi 1967; Shefter 1977). In fragmented states, governmental units may have overlapping and conflicting jurisdiction. This makes power more diffuse, as any specific unit is likely to have difficulty realizing its policy vision. Permeability means it is possible for social interests (e.g. trade unions and business associations) outside the state to influence government policy, and when there are multiple points of entry, these interests can try to influence policy by making contact with the diverse range of governmental actors involved in the policy of interest. Again, this diffuses power at one level, but it also makes it possible for interests with greater economic resources and informal connections to governmental officials to influence policy-making (Domhoff 1983). By contrast, of course, in less fragmented systems where policy-making is more centralized and there is less permeability, governmental units responsible for specific policies are relatively more powerful – more able to enact their policy agendas.

Political parties in the US lack programs to which elected party members are required to adhere. In addition, there is no requirement that elected officials vote a party line in Congress, for example. US political parties have difficulty disciplining their recalcitrant members. Thus, these parties have a relatively limited capacity to enact their vision. They are not very powerful. By contrast, political parties – generally in parliamentary systems – that are able to enforce discipline are better able to enact their programs. They are more powerful.

Finally, take a more macro or general case still: gender. Gender itself can be understood as a social structure. Judith Lorber understands gender as a structure "that establishes patterns of expectations for individuals, orders the social processes of everyday life, is built into the major social organizations of society, such as the economy, ideology, the family, and politics, and is also an entity in and of itself" (1994: 1). At the most general level, there are no formal rules defining gender relations. Instead, they are typically informal but deeply entrenched, and create a stratified system in which, in general, women experience more constraints and men more opportunities.

I understand power in terms of capacity and constraint. We must consider how formal and informal "rules of play" make possible certain actions and the realization of certain goals by some actors, while making the actions of other actors and the realization of their goals less likely. A professor's formal position may make the realization of her goals as against a student's more likely. But it may not be just the formal rules that define the professor's position in the laboratory and university, but a host of resources that are associated with that position. The professor's grants may pay to run the laboratory. Here is an empowering economic resource. But in addition, the professor has pivotal cultural resources – the informal system of classification that allows her to know in an unthinking way what it means to be and behave like a scientist (Bourdieu 1984). Another component of the professor's cultural resources is the unreflected-upon assumptions about the rights and abilities of the scientist.

To this point, I have distinguished economic and cultural resources. Again, this is ultimately an analytical distinction, not something that exists intrinsically in society. "Economic" refers to financial resources that can be used to enable some actors and constrain others. "Cultural" refers to norms, beliefs, and values that may be drawn upon consciously or unconsciously and thereby define opportunities and constraints. This notion of cultural resource is closely related to the way in which I will use discourse. The realm of discourse is the sphere of meaning. It is a thoroughly social realm from which the categories through which we make sense of the world come.

The discursive terrain is not constituted by a singular discourse. Instead, it is made up of overlapping and often contradictory discourses (S. Hall 1982). But although there are always secondary or subordinate discourses, generally it is dominant discourses that define what is sayable and what is a legitimate. Whether articulated consciously or not, dominant discourses are the most efficacious resources. They provide a kind of cultural authority to actors who deploy them (Schatzberg 1999: 5). The power of these discourses is greatly enhanced by the extent to which the truth of their basic claims is taken for granted (Meyer & Rowan 1977; Kleinman & Kloppenburg 1991; Schatzberg 1999). Actors draw on a particular set of discourses, and those with historical resonance and deep social legitimacy are the ones that are likely to hold the discursive high ground, eclipsing discourses that lack historical force and consequently legitimacy (Kleinman & Kloppenburg 1991; see also P. Hall 1986). In fact, actors pursuing a line of argument that challenges the dominant discourse will often attempt to manipulate that discourse in a way that can increase the legitimacy of their position (Kleinman & Kloppenburg 1991). They will use a dominant discourse to make their case.

I should make a couple of closing remarks about viewing the social world as a world thoroughly infused by power. A focus on power does not imply that social actors always act strategically and self-consciously to achieve their ends. One can imagine, for example, a small group of citizens appointed by a local government to make policy recommendations on biotechnology gathering to discuss the issues at stake. One can imagine further that all participants were formally equal. In this context, however, gender norms could result in men speaking more often and more determinedly and consequently having more of their points win the day. In addition, the taken for granted beliefs about the validity of expertise (call this a discourse of expertise) could lead some members of this group of citizens to unquestioningly accept the views of "certified experts" on the citizen body, whose opinion would then win the day. In this example, participating actors may not conclude that one group emerged victorious over another. However, as analysts we may conclude that the social organization of power – here understood in terms of gender and a discourse of expertise – shaped the outcome of this situation.

A second point I need to make concerns the status of "social construction." I believe, with many in the social sciences and humanities writing today, that the social world is constructed. But I differ with those who focus only on the processes of construction themselves – that is, with those who explore how, for example, gender, race, or science is constructed at site "x." I believe this is important work; however, it is also the case that our social world is relatively stable. At any given point in time, the already established features of that world – factors that have been constructed over time – serve to define the opportunities and constraints faced by actors. They shape actors's practices and the outcomes of social struggles, policies, and programs. In this book I am interested, then, in how relatively stable features of our social world shape practices, struggles, policies, and programs in the realm of technoscience.

NOTES

1   When I use the term "discourse," I do so in the limited sense of "systems of symbolic meaning codified in language that influence how actors observe, interpret, and reason in particular social settings" (Campbell & Pedersen 2001: 9). On scientism and technological progressivism see Kleinman and Kinchy (2003a and 2003b).
2   Kleinman (2000a) provides a number of cases that powerfully contradict this claim.
3   For a view of Luddites as thoughtful critics, see Noble (1984).
4   Recent research has shown this case to be more complicated than Winner's portrayal suggests (see Joerges 1999). But as Sismondo points out, there is a slew of other cases that make Winner's point. Thus, Sismondo suggests that speed bumps serve a political purpose. They reduce and slow traffic and simultaneously increase the property values of family-oriented neighborhoods where they are installed (2004: 80). Such speed bumps embody the interest of home owners over those attempting to maneuver through the streets efficiently.

2

Ceding Debate: Biotechnology and Agriculture

The US and global economies are in the midst of a massive transformation. A complete outline of the new economies that will emerge is by no means certain, but some of the central characteristics of the new economies are clear. Many countries in the northern hemisphere are moving away from their post-Second World War foundation in heavy industry, and to some extent, the smokestack firms that remain are replacing rigid mass-production models with various forms of flexible organization (see Kenney & Florida 1993; Graham 1995). Much unskilled work is being farmed out to countries in the southern hemisphere. At the same time, the US and other western countries are shifting increasingly to a high-technology, knowledge-intensive mode of production. The industries that feature centrally in this new economy are information technology and biotechnology (see Kleinman & Vallas 2001).

These two engines of economic growth mean different things for countries in the north and the south. For highly industrialized nations, while creating new social class cleavages, these sectors promise increases in economic efficiency and productivity. They could lead to reductions in pollution, improved transportation safety, life saving drugs, and new foods. For countries in the south, the advantages of the new economy are less clear; disputes about ownership of biological materials crucial to the economic revolution underway, dangerous working conditions in firms owned by US- or Europe-based multinationals, and growing disparities of wealth and access to new technologies cloud optimistic visions of a high-tech future.

Consideration of the broad social impacts of the emerging new knowledge economy could fill several volumes. In this book, I will consider a limited number of what I consider to be some of the most important societal implications of recent developments in this "new world order." In this chapter, I begin with biotechnology. Here again, the topic is vast, and I will restrict myself to consideration of agricultural biotechnology. The chapter is divided into three primary sections. In the first, I provide a general introduction to biotechnology and the structure of American agriculture. In the next sections, I consider how recent developments in biotechnology are affecting the social organization of agriculture. Here, most of my attention is directed at farming and the relationship between farming and agribusiness. I look primarily at the United States, with some attention to Europe. Issues of control, power, and social division are central to my discussion. To some extent, I consider biotechnology in the southern hemisphere in chapter 4. In the final section of the chapter, I look at the way in which the public controversy over agricultural biotechnology has been framed by the proponents and opponents of the technology, and I explore some of the implications of this framing. Here, I pay special attention to the discourses of scientism and technological progressivism, which I discussed in chapter 1.

BIOTECHNOLOGY AND THE SOCIAL ORGANIZATION OF AGRICULTURE AND AGRIBUSINESS

Introduction

What is biotechnology? Definitions of biotechnology vary, but central to all descriptions is recombinant DNA (rDNA). A technique developed in the early 1970s by Stanley Cohen of Stanford University and Herbert Boyer of the University of California – San Francisco, rDNA can be understood as a method for isolating and making multiple copies of a DNA segment or entire gene and for moving DNA from one organism and combining it with genetic material from another. What makes this technology revolutionary is the possibility it creates to circumvent "natural" barriers of biological incompatibility. That is, rDNA makes it possible to combine genetic material from two different species of animal or even to combine genetic material of a plant with that of an animal or bacterium (Kloppenburg & Kenney 1984: 5). The series of important breakthroughs that followed in the early years after Cohen and Boyer's discovery include: the first rDNA-based animal vaccine (approved for use in Europe in 1981), the first rDNA pharmaceutical product (human insulin approved for use in the US and Great Britain in 1982), the first expression of a plant gene in a different species of plant (1983), the creation of the first transgenic animal (a mouse created in 1988 with genes from another species), and the introduction of a foreign gene into a human (1989).

One could imagine biotechnology being developed in a variety of ways in the agricultural context. It might be used primarily as a supplementary tool by researchers seeking to understand agriculture as part of a larger biological system and hoping to use traditional plant breeding to develop a low-input, but highly productive, farm sector. It might be utilized to build on an already productive chemical-intensive agricultural system of questionable sustainability. In this context, the technique might be deployed in the service of companies aiming to control their products, and researchers might be attentive primarily to the role of individual genes and not to agriculture as part of a larger biological system.

The many possible routes of development are social choices, but they are choices constrained by social structures which give certain actors more power than others in shaping the trajectory that technology will take. As well, technological development along an existing trajectory will proceed based on contours established by the existing history of technological development. In this context, even subordinate actors (say, family farmers as opposed to large agrichemical corporations) may have real economic as well as ideological commitments to the existing path.

In terms of understanding how agricultural biotechnology has developed to date, several aspects of the social organization of agriculture prior to the advent of biotechnology should be borne in mind. First, ongoing efforts to promote sustained productivity gains are a central feature of the modern history of US agriculture. US agricultural productivity gains are underpinned by an array of developments in science and technology. Combined with developments in plant breeding, agricultural chemicals introduced in the period after the Second World War substantially increased agricultural yields (Perkins 1982; Harrington 1996). From the end of the Second World War through the first part of the 1960s, for example, corn production per acre nearly doubled from some 36.5 bushels per acre to over 68. In wheat, to take another case, productivity rose from 16 bushels per acre to nearly 26 (Kohn 1987). These productivity increases came with a substantial rise in agrichemical use. Between 1947 and 1960, synthetic pesticide production increased five times and had reached nearly two billion pounds annually by 1981 (Doyle 1985: 183). By 1991, US farmers were spending close to two billion dollars on insecticides, herbicides, and fungicides (Palladino 1996: 8). Thus, many US farmers have come to expect productivity gains and to assume that the means to these productivity improvements is agrichemicals – always new and improved.

As US farmers became more dependent on purchased inputs – seeds and chemicals – in the period after the Second World War, the structure of agriculture was undergoing a dramatic change. From 1915 to 1945, the number of farmers in the US declined by only 8 percent, but between 1945 and 1975, there was a 55 percent drop in the number of US farms from 5.9 million to 2.8 million (Busch et al. 1991). By 1999, there were fewer than two million farmers in the US, and the vast bulk of all farm receipts were received by only 6 percent of farms, primarily large "super farms" (Lacy 2000).

As fewer farms produce an increasingly large percentage of our food, a similar trend is occurring in agribusiness. In the mid-1970s, there were some 30 US companies developing pesticides, but only 12 by the late 1980s. At the same time, the division between seed companies and pesticide producers is blurring as mergers and takeovers become the order of the day (Busch et al. 1991). Equally, agriculture is dominated not by small-scale farmers but by companies that sell farm inputs and processes and those that package and market food. And it is these firms that benefit disproportionately from the transformation that has occurred over the past century, and have had and will continue to have a disproportionate role in determining the future of agriculture.[1]

Herbicide resistant crops and technology protection systems

In just a few short years, biotechnology has spread like wildfire across the farming landscape in the US and worldwide. In 1997, just 15 percent of the US soybean crop was from genetically engineered seed. By 1998, the figure had grown to 44 percent, and by 2001 the figure was roughly two-thirds (Simon 2001). According to one source, across the globe, between 1996 and 2002, the total area planted in genetically modified crops increased from less than 2 million acres to some 145 million acres, and the byproducts of GMOs are found in around 70 percent of processed foods sold in the United States (Kloppenburg 2004). Jack Kloppenburg speculates that "Since high fructose corn syrup, and soy, cotton, and canola oils are ingredients in a high proportion of processed foods, nearly every resident of the United States has probably consumed food stuffs containing GMOs or their products" (2004).

What is the nature of these crops and what do they mean for the character of agriculture? Looking at early corporate promotional material, one might be excused for coming away with an inaccurate impression. In a newspaper advertisement from the mid-1980s paid for by the Monsanto Corporation, a single stalk of corn is pictured growing in a parched landscape; the ground is cracked, the stalk appears to be the only thing living. Although the ad's text does not explicitly say that biotechnology will allow crops to grow where none have grown before, or that it will enable us to feed the hungry, that is clearly the impression, and other promotional materials do say as much. According to a 1999 Monsanto brochure, "Population is increasing rapidly worldwide, yet the amount of arable land available for the production of food is diminishing. In order to produce enough food, farmers everywhere will need crop plants that are high yielding and require fewer inputs, such as insecticides, fertilizers and herbicides" (1999: 3). In contrast to the image presented in corporate promotional materials, according to one study, "Research on some of the traits most needed in the developing world such as the ability to tolerate low soil fertility, the ability to tolerate soil salinity or alkalinity, and techniques for producing biological pesticides has gone unstudied" (Lacy 2000: 86).

The reality is that companies working on agricultural biotech need to make a profit, and poor farmers, especially those in the southern hemisphere, are not likely to fill corporate coffers. Monsanto was one of the early and is probably the most prominent investor in agricultural biotech research. Today, more than 90 percent of transgenic plants grown worldwide depend on Monsanto seed technology (Simon 2001). But according to Daniel Charles, in the early days, the company was confronted over and over again by a persistent question: how could biotech be made profitable? By 1992, Monsanto's senior management told its research staff that they wanted evidence that biotech could produce value for the company by the year's end, or the company's commitment would need to be radically scaled back (Charles 2001: 112). It turned out that the way to make money was not to develop drought-resistant crops or plants that would thrive under conditions of low soil fertility or high soil salinity or alkalinity. Instead, the company developed seed that tied farmers in the US and Europe tightly to the company and that reinforced the model of chemical agriculture that already dominates crop production in the US and elsewhere. In a prescient 1984 article, Jack Kloppenburg and Martin Kenney predicted that agribusiness would increase overall control of agricultural production through the nexus of the seed, and genetically engineered herbicide resistant crops (HRCs), among the biggest selling genetically modified crops (GMCs), do just that. Herbicide resistant seeds are genetically engineered to be able to survive the spraying of specific herbicides. In the age of chemical pesticides, it was typically the case that farmers could only use herbicides to kill the weeds in their fields before crop plants emerged from the surface of the earth. Today, with HRCs, farmers can apply herbicides after plants have broken the topsoil. The herbicide will kill surrounding weeds, but the engineered crop will be spared.

As Krimsky and Wrubel note, "A company will gain substantially if it can increase the market share for a herbicide to which it holds the patent. By creating crops resistant to its herbicide a company can expand markets for its patented chemicals" (Krimsky & Wrubel 1996: 35). This innovation means that to get the most out of a company's herbicide a farmer needs to purchase both crop seed and herbicide from a single company.

The US agricultural market for herbicides was nearly 4 billion dollars annually by the mid-1990s, a figure that substantially exceeds sales of insecticides and fungicides (Krimsky & Wrubel 1996: 35). And according to one source, two-thirds of the genetically engineered crops available in 1999 were "designed specifically to increase the sale of herbicides and pesticides produced by the companies selling the genetically engineered seeds" (Lacy 2000: 82).

Since the 1970s, Monsanto's leading agricultural product has been the glyphosate-based herbicide known as Roundup. Developing crops that could tolerate glyphosate was a way to boost Roundup sales. Crop plants resistant to Roundup would survive herbicide spraying and make possible more effective weed control (Simon 2001: A18). And farmers interested in controlling their weeds more effectively and efficiently would have to purchase both seeds and herbicide from Monsanto or its licensees. According to Simon, "Since the introduction of Roundup Ready crops, glyphosate use has soared. It was applied on 20% of US farm acreage in 1995; four years later, on 62%." There are several brands of glyphosate herbicide, but the boom has been especially profitable for Monsanto. Roundup sales were $2.6 million in 2000 (Simon 2001: A18), and herbicide-tolerant crops account for nearly 80 percent of the total worldwide area plant in genetically modified seed.[2]

We see two things clearly in this case. First, development of biotechnology appears to follow the existing agrichemical trajectory, and secondly, Monsanto's market domination has forcefully allowed the company to shape this path. In this context, since profitability is the primary criterion for corporate sponsored agricultural research, it is not surprising that through the end of 1995 most industry research aimed not specifically to increase output but to create herbicide and insect resistant crops (Lacy 2000: 86). And the crops on which research was undertaken were those that would likely return substantial profits and not those – minor crops in industrialized countries and all crops in third world countries – for which there are weed problems for which there is currently no adequate solution (Krimsky & Wrubel 1996: 50, 46, 47).

From a sociological perspective, a central issue raised by HRCs is control. Who controls the seed and thus agricultural practice? There are two ways in which the HRCs shift the balance of control from the farmer to the company. First, while in earlier periods farmers might have selected crops and pest control technology, with HRCs the two come as a package purchased from a single company. Second, HRCs are, as I have noted, patented technologies, and farmers must have licenses to use them. Traditionally, farmers planted crop seed and then they would save a certain portion of their seed for planting in the next season. But companies like Monsanto require farmers who purchase their seed to sign a contract that forbids the farmer from saving seed from harvest for planting in the future. To prevent farmers from illegally saving seed, Monsanto has developed what might be termed a divide and conquer strategy. The company operates a toll-free telephone line that encourages competing farmers to turn their neighbors in if they have evidence of illegal planting. With this evidence, Monsanto can use its disproportionate economic power to force farmers to conform to the company's rules. Importantly, of course, the rules are not just the company's. While seed saving might be a traditional practice, Monsanto has the widely accepted values of intellectual property law on its side (see chapter 6).

Monsanto has received hundreds of calls. The company has asked farmers caught violating the agreement they signed to pay a fine. But in addition, the firm has taken a number of farmers to court. Among them is Mitchell Scruggs, a soy and cotton farmer from Mississippi. Scruggs openly defied the contract, believing that he has a right to save some of his harvest for replanting. When the Mississippi farmer was sued by Monsanto, he counter-sued charging the company had violated antitrust law, colluding with seed companies and retailers and hurting farmers. According to Scruggs, "They're trying to control all the food and fiber in the world by monopolizing the seed industry" (quoted in Simon 2001: A19).

While not as long as the history of farm seed saving, agribusiness has an extended history of working to control farmer use of and access to agricultural inputs. Hybrid seed developed by Pioneer Hi-Bred in the 1930s is an early innovation in this tradition (Kloppenburg 2004). These seeds, while more productive than their open-pollinated predecessors, are economically sterile. That is, planting the offspring of hybrid crop plants results in a substantial reduction in yield. If hybrids were a biological means to force farmers back to market annually, legal means have also been utilized. In 1970, seed companies saw passage of the US Plant Variety Protection Act, a law that gives seed companies ownership over seed produced from plants grown from a company's own legally protected seed.

HRCs expand the range of control by linking seed and herbicide, but the mechanism of control is ultimately legal, not biological. It is Monsanto's threat of lawsuit that is the means by which the company hopes to retain control over its new seed/herbicide packages. By contrast, a new biological system, called a "technology protection system" by its developers and "terminator technology" by its critics, returns the agricultural system to the type of control made possible by hybrid varieties. Using genetic engineering techniques, scientists affiliated with the US Department of Agriculture and a small firm called Delta and Pine developed a means to make farm-saved seed sterile. Like hybrid varieties this mechanism could make seed saving virtually impossible and require farmers to return to the market each year to purchase new seed. According to one source, every major seed and agrichemical firm is developing a version of this technology (Pesticide Action Network 1999). These technology protection systems allow companies breeding new seed to control the use of that material, but by engineering seeds so that the terminator mechanism is turned on and off through the application of a given company's patented chemical, these systems make possible enhanced control of the agricultural production process by corporate concerns.

Although developers of various types of technology protection systems contend that this technology could serve a useful social function by preventing the spread of domesticated genetic material into the wild environment (Pesticide Action Network 1999), critics are dubious (Brac de al Perriere & Seuret 2000: 29), and Monsanto is clear that this new technology will allow the company to protect its investment (Brac de la Perriere & Seuret 2000: 27). This point is reinforced by a USDA spokesman who described their patented system as a way of preventing "unauthorized use of American technology" (quoted in ETC Group 2002: 3). This USDA official said that their technology protection system will "increase the value of proprietary seed owned by US seed companies and open up new markets in Second and Third World countries"(quoted in ETC Group 2002: 3). In the face of widespread criticism of the terminator technology, in 1999, Monsanto agreed not to commercialize this specific invention, but the company said it intended to continue development of systems that will make it possible to turn on and off genetic targets crucial to a given crop's productivity. In addition, with other companies developing similar tools, the use anticipated by critics and described by corporate and government officials seems likely.

To reiterate, what we see here is technological development consistent with an existing trajectory. As I have suggested, other paths were possible, but the one down which we have come is not only consistent with the existing social organization of agriculture, but with the interests of the most powerful actors in the system: agrichemical firms. And to protect their interests, these firms can draw on an established and widely accepted system of intellectual property protection and use their disproportionate economic resources to enforce their rights under law.

Recombinant Bovine Growth Hormone: the first product of agricultural biotechnology

Recombinant Bovine Growth Hormone (rBGH), often called recombinant Bovine Somatotropin (rBST), is a very different technology than herbicide resistant crops and technology protection systems. The social issue here is not so much about increased corporate control as about perpetuating a technology treadmill in which the market pushes farmers to adopt the latest technology, exacerbates competition, pushes prices down, and forces a sectoral restructuring in which small-scale family farms are most likely to be casualties and larger, managerially more sophisticated farms are likely to survive. In short, this technology is likely to reinforce existing trends toward sectoral concentration, at a time when the need for increased production is debatable at best.

Somatotropin is a hormone produced by the anterior pituitary gland in mammals. Somatotropin plays a role in mammal milk production, and researchers in the 1920s found that lactating laboratory animals treated with the hormone had increased milk yield. In the 1930s, injections of the hormone given to lactating cows produced similar results. The amounts of naturally produced BGH or BST were insufficient to permit scientists to treat cows with the substance in a way that would provide sustained and widespread increases in milk yield. However, when it became possible to produce BGH microbially using recombinant DNA techniques, several companies, including Monsanto, worked to produce a marketable product. In 1993, the US Food and Drug Administration approved the use of one form of rBGH (Krimsky & Wrubel 1996: 167, 168). Several other countries, however, have banned its use (see below).

Early analysts of rBGH speculated that the technology would not be scale neutral – that is, that larger farms would more easily and successfully adopt the technology and would undersell smaller dairy operations. Subsequent debate leaves open the question of whether the technology is scale neutral, but it is certainly the case that "once management practices are factored in to the scale issue expert opinion leans heavily toward the conclusion that large herds will benefit more from BST" than small herds (Krimsky & Wrubel 1996: 181). In other words, it is not size *per se* that will advantage larger dairy operations, but managerial sophistication. Larger dairies are more likely than smaller farms to have fully integrated computer monitoring systems into their production regime, and this is likely to help them make the most of rBGH.

The long-term effects of rBGH on the structure of dairy farming cannot be ascertained with certainty at this writing, but recent research on the Wisconsin dairy industry confirms early speculation. Based on a statewide random sample mail survey with a response rate of about 50 percent, Barham, Jackson-Smith, and Moon conclude that: "rBST adoption in Wisconsin in 1999 has a dramatic size-bias, with the average adopting farm having well more than twice the mean herd-size of the non-adopters." The use of sophisticated farm management strategies is also a strong predictor of rBGH adoption in Wisconsin (2001: 16).

From a sociological perspective, the rBGH case challenges the aspect of technological progressivism that suggests that new technology is always and everywhere beneficent. This technology is likely to reinforce existing trends toward a highly stratified system of agricultural production. From a political perspective, at a time when dairy production in the US and Europe is ample to meet demand, it seems worth questioning the social appropriateness of a technology that may exacerbate surpluses and put small scale producers out of business.

Bacillus thuringiensis and "genetic drift"

In the previous two sections, we have seen how the push of corporate profits has driven agricultural biotechnology research in a direction that undermines farmer control over production processes and has led away from the rapid introduction of drought resistant crops and plants that would survive in low fertility soil. We have also seen how the introduction of a new biotechnology (rBGH) may reinforce trends toward fewer and larger farm operations. In this section, I consider an additional largely *indirect* effect of agribusiness biotechnology development by a powerful agrichemical industry on small-scale producers. In the cases discussed below, the issue is whether corporate practices will hurt organic producers, where these producers are not purchasing genetically engineered inputs.

Bacillus thuringiensis (*Bt*) is a common soil bacterium. It produces proteins that have highly specific insecticidal activity. One group of the proteins is toxic to caterpillars, while another is toxic to beetle larvae (Krimsky & Wrubel 1996: 56). *Bt* was discovered to be toxic to the silk moth in Japan in 1902. However, the mechanism of toxicity was not determined until the 1950s. Since 1958, however, *Bt*-based formulas have been available for use by farmers and home gardeners. *Bt*'s selectivity, apparent lack of short- or long-term toxicity to animals, and the ability to apply the substance just before harvest are seen as important advantages of *Bt* over many chemical insecticides (Krimsky & Wrubel 1996: 56), and this substance has been highly prized, especially by organic farmers and gardeners.

More recently, however, researchers have transferred relevant genes from *Bt* to crop plants in order to create crops that produce their own insect toxins, and in May of 1995, the US Environmental Protection Agency approved commercial release of *Bt* potatoes. Produced by Monsanto, this was the first commercial release of transgenic crop plants containing a pesticide. The aim was to control the Colorado potato beetle (Krimsky & Wrubel 1996: 60). Any crop on which *Bt* spray can be used can be genetically engineered to produce the *Bt* toxin itself. In addition to field crops, like potatoes and corn, companies are currently attempting to develop *Bt* fruit trees (Jenkins 1998: 17). Since these early efforts, *Bt* crops have spread rapidly in US agriculture. In 1996, *Bt* maize accounted for less than one percent of US production. By 1998, the percentage was 19 (Jenkins 1998: 18).

The development of this technology has created dissension among some in the environmental movement and among organic farmers. Crop plants are part of an ecosystem including the pests they confront. Ultimately, pests develop resistance to whatever pesticides are widely used. Some argue that the development of resistance to the *Bt* endotoxin would be particularly slow were the substance only sprayed onto plants the way it has been since the 1950s, because the *Bt* spray is used only occasionally and degrades quickly. But some environmentalists and sustainable agriculture advocates worry that resistance may develop more rapidly where the toxin is part of the plant itself as a result of genetic engineering (Krimsky & Wrubel 1996: 63, 64).

The industry argues that *Bt* could "easily be bred to produce thousands of strains and so keep ahead of the resistant insects" (Jenkins 1998: 15). However, there is evidence that "insects resistant to one strain of *Bt* could also be resistant to other strains, even those with which they had never been in contact" (Jenkins 1998: 16). In California, according to Jenkins, widespread use of *Bt* sprays already threatens to promote widespread resistance (1998: 16).

Scientists and others have argued for the creation of refuges that buffer fields on which *Bt* crops are grown. These refuges would allow *Bt* vulnerable insects to multiply and reduce the rate at which *Bt*-resistant insects come to dominate insect populations (Jenkins 1998: 18). Companies support this idea, but some critics of this technology contend that "the refuge strategies proposed will extend the useful life of Bt by [not] more than a few years" (Jenkins 1998: 18).

Whether or not refuge strategies extend the life of *Bt*, we have a case here where ultimately corporate domination of agricultural pest control products may serve to effectively remove a successful tool utilized by farmers who deviate from the traditional postwar agricultural model. Companies are not actively engaging in efforts to control the production practices of farmers, in the same way in which herbicide resistant crops and "terminator technologies" effectively do. Agribusiness firms are not explicitly stealing this tool, thus forcing organic producers to turn to the dominant model. But by enhancing the rate at which pests develop resistance to *Bt*, the biotechnological strategy Monsanto and other firms are following will indirectly affect the production practices of organic producers.

The problem of "genetic drift" raises related issues. "Genetic drift" refers to cross-pollination between biotech crops and nonbiotech crops from separate fields. Insects, birds, and wind spread pollen from genetically modified organisms to fields planted with conventional and organic seed, and the drift can occur across many miles. Contamination of organic crops can also occur through the sharing of equipment, like combines, elevators, and trucks.

There have been a number of suspected cases of "genetic drift." In 1998, "genetic drift" is believed to have contaminated organic corn in Texas. According to Anthony Shadid, "The contamination was not discovered until the corn had been processed and shipped to Europe as organic tortilla chips under the brand name Apache. When testing revealed traces of biotech corn, the shipment of 87,000 bags was recalled, costing the company more than $150,000" (Shadid 2001: G1). In 2000, Nebraska farmer David Vetter found biotech contamination of his organic corn (Lilliston 2001). And although Susan and Mark Fitzgerald, who farm outside of Hancock, Minnesota, set up barriers to stop "genetic drift" – bushes, shrubs, and trees – a recent harvest revealed contamination of their organic corn crop by GMO – Bt corn. They had to take 800 bushels off the organic market at a cost of $2,000 (Shadid 2001). In April 2001, the Wall Street Journal tested 20 food products labeled "GMO free." Of these, 16 were found to contain at least traces of GMO ingredients (Lilliston 2001).

The problem of "genetic drift" is similar to the case of Bt. Here, commercial manufacturers of genetically engineered crops are not actively trying to undermine the organic status of organic producers. But in this case, agribusiness domination of the crop seed market and an agricultural landscape that reflects that domination mean it is virtually impossible for organic producers to guarantee a GMO-free crop. Indeed, according to some analysts, virtually all commercial seed has some level of genetically modified proteins, only a few short years after GM crops were introduced commercially (Shadid 2001: G1). And while federal regulations require buffer zones around genetically modified crops to protect the integrity of other crops, this 660-foot area has proved insufficient (Shadid 2001).

Where does this leave farmers who do not utilize GM crops, especially organic producers? Insurance companies say they do not cover genetic contamination, and it is not clear whether farmers using GM crops and companies producing them can be held liable for contamination due to "genetic drift." Given the legal wherewithal of major agribusiness concerns, it seems unlikely they will be held liable, and thus these firms's domination of US agriculture is likely to continue to indirectly threaten small niche alternatives.

The cases considered in this section contradict the basic themes that underpin the discourse of technological progressivism. First, technologies clearly do not proceed automatically down a single path. Here, the boundaries of the path have been shaped by the post-Second World War history of US agriculture, and evidence that corporate investment in research has been directed toward such initiatives as herbicide resistant plants and not, for example, toward developing crops that could tolerate low soil fertility or high soil salinity or techniques for producing biological pesticides suggests that with a different research agenda other paths might be possible. Second, the idea that technology development is always and universally beneficent is clearly mistaken. Advantage from the development of new technologies is often stratified: some actors reap rewards, and others lose out. This is made clear by the rBGH case, where managerially more sophisticated farmers and the companies manufacturing the substance are likely to benefit most from the technology. The cases of *Bt* plants and "genetic drift" also illustrate that the benefits from new technologies can be stratified. Here, while the farmers who use genetically engineered plants might benefit and the companies that produce them surely will, farmers who wish to avoid them will be hurt through more rapid development of pest resistance and contamination of non-GM crops by pollen from genetically engineered plants.

These cases illustrate further that artifacts – what we think of as technologies – embody values. In the cases of biotechnological agricultural products, the values centrally implicated are those that undergird chemical-intensive postwar agriculture. Furthermore, these technologies reflect the interests first and foremost of the agribusiness concerns – Monsanto, especially – that were responsible for developing them. To put it simply, Roundup Ready seed has increased Monsanto's sales of Roundup.

Finally, these cases can be usefully understood by utilizing the notion of power I outlined in chapter 1. First, the path of technological development in the case of agricultural biotechnologies by and large reflects the existing structure (chemical-intensive agriculture). This is an instance where an aspect of the social world has been shaped by stable attributes of it. Furthermore, financial resources enable companies like Monsanto to promote a research agenda that will serve their interests and to reinforce their research decisions with threats of litigation. Finally, the companies's position is bolstered by an established legal discourse – a set of laws (intellectual property laws) that work in their interests.

THE DISCURSIVE LANDSCAPE IN
THE DEBATE OVER BIOTECHNOLOGY

Beyond the established legal discourse, proponents of the kind of agricultural biotechnology that has been commercialized so far have benefited in the US and to a lesser extent elsewhere from occupying the discursive high ground. That is, their interests can be furthered best by drawing on the social common sense – those ideas about the way the social world works that are so taken for granted that we unthinkingly accept them. In this section, I explore the discursive terrain in debates over the development of biotechnology as these have been carried on in the US Congress, in

European Union policy-making bodies, and in promotional efforts of proponents and opponents of biotechnology.

Early debates about biotechnology in the US Congress[3]

We can see the discourses I described in chapter 1 – scientism and technological progressivism – at work in the early policy debates over biotechnology in the US Congress. The 1975 Asilomar Conference marked a pivotal point in biotechnology policy debate. Scientism fundamentally guided the boundaries of discussion and the claims made at this conference. Asilomar embodied the basic principle that scientific development is a technical matter for scientists to assess without public intervention. According to Sheldon Krimsky, "In the critical planning period of Asilomar, the controversy over rDNA research was reduced to a set of technical problems related to biohazards in the research laboratory" (1982: 99). Indeed, Krimsky argues that the issues at Asilomar were defined in such a way that qualification to participate in discussion remained the monopoly of scientists (1982: 153), and Asilomar set the framework within which early Congressional debate over biotechnology occurred.

When the first Congressional hearing on rDNA research occurred in April of 1975, Stanley Cohen, one of the developers of rDNA technology, made it clear in his testimony that "ethical issues are quite peripheral to ... biological safety questions," which are the central matters for consideration by policy-makers (US Senate 1975: 2). The power of scientism in this hearing is made clearer still by the fact that even a critic of the standard scientist position argued not that the line between facts and values is blurred on these matters (how much is safe enough? What is a good measure of safety?), but only that the public should give scientists informed consent (US Senate 1975: 14).

By 1983, Congressional attention in the US turned from human protection during rDNA research to the potential environmental hazards of the deliberate release of genetically engineered organisms as part of agricultural research. Despite a change in the substantive focus of the hearings and indeed a broadening of debate participants, the terrain of discussion remained similar. The problem to be resolved was framed as a technical matter of determining appropriate scientific criteria of risk (US House of Representatives 1983).

Moving beyond scientism, a discourse we might term free marketism – the idea that markets should decide what technologies are developed and how – entered Congressional debate in 1984 as the commercial potential of rDNA technology for agriculture became clear. Corporate representatives and government officials warned members of Congress against imposing "overly restrictive" regulations that might hurt the ability of US firms to compete internationally (US Senate 1984). Let the market work, seemed to be the essential claim.

The discursive terrain in the rBGH debate:
The US and the European Union

By the mid-1980s, public controversy over biotechnology in both Europe and the US centered on rBGH. The first product of genetic engineering to be considered for commercial release, rBGH was the focus of a storm of debate among farmers, consumers, the dairy industry, and proponents of biotechnology. In 1986, the US House of Representatives held the Congress's first hearing on rBGH, and the terrain of discussion was largely bounded by an extension of free marketism and a clearly articulated technological progressivism. Several witnesses rejected the idea that policy-makers should be concerned about the potential impact of the commercialization of rBGH on the structure of family farming in the US. Instead, proponents of the new technology argued that efficient farmers would benefit from rBGH, but it would not "turn an inefficient manager into an efficient one" (US House of Representatives 1986: 8). The presumed implication of this line of argument is that the market should select between the efficient and inefficient farmer.

The inherent value of progress embodied in rBGH came out clearly in these hearings as well. As one trade association representative noted, rBGH is "just the latest generation of change that has placed the American dairy industry on the leading edge of productivity improvements" (US House of Representatives 1986: 189). rBGH is just one technology in a path of constant improvement, according to this line of thinking. The inevitability of technological progress was made clear in this hearing by several speakers who, like Representative Jim Jeffords, noted that "we can't really stand in the way of progress" (US House of Representatives 1986: 16). Finally, the way in which a dominant discourse – here technological progressivism – establishes what appears reasonable came out clearly in a statement by Representative Tony Coelho, who chaired the session. He said "I would like to . . . make one clarifying statement; that is, I don't think any of us are [sic] against scientific progress" (US House of Representatives 1986: 4).

This is not to say that alternative discourses were not deployed by participants in these debates. Critics of rBGH drew on what is clearly a subordinate discourse in the US context: a language that points to the ways in which decisions about technology embody values and have social effects – that is, a language that contradicts technological progressivism, suggesting that some technologies should not be developed.

The path leading to federal approval of rBGH for use in the US actually began before the 1986 hearing, and issues of the socioeconomic impacts of this technology were significant in bringing the matter to public attention. In 1984, Robert Kalter, an economist at Cornell University, published a study in which he concluded that 30 percent of dairy farmers would go out of business within 5 years of the approval of rBGH (Collier 2000: 157). Other studies published in the late 1980s and early 1990s suggested that rBGH would reinforce or accelerate the structural transformation of the US dairy industry away from small-scale producers (Office of Technology Assessment 1991).

In the US, many of the most vocal opponents of rBGH, particularly in the debates in the mid-1980s, based their opposition to the drug on socioeconomic concerns. One analysis suggests that criticism of rBGH based on socioeconomic concerns had an important influence in government regulatory bodies, turning rBGH into a dairy policy issue (Browne & Hamm 1988). Concerns about the survival of the family farm, combined with worries that an increase in milk supplies would overburden the federal dairy support program, were effective in mobilizing a grassroots movement against rBGH.

In 1989, critics of the new technology petitioned the US Food and Drug Administration (FDA), asking the agency to study, among other things, the socioeconomic impacts of rBGH (Sinclair 1986). In that same year, Wisconsin and Minnesota passed moratoria on the use of the substance in those states. In both cases, opponents of the technology were concerned about its potential socioeconomic impacts, but also expressed fears about rBGH's human and animal health effects.

Clearly a subordinate discourse lacking the historical resonance of scientism and technological determinism, although drawn on by some rBGH critics, this social discourse was never central to public policy debate over the substance in the US. It was never seriously considered by policy-makers as a basis for regulating the new technology, and it never found its way into policy proposals in the US (or at the state level). Instead, the ultimate approval of commercialization of rBGH in the US, which came in 1993, was rooted in technological progressivism and scientism. Proponents of the drug used the rhetoric of technological progress, scientism, and free market efficiency to gain American support and delegitimize criticism based on such "emotional" issues as the negative impact rBGH would have on family farms.

The discursive terrain on which debate over the development of rBGH occurred in the European Union was considerably different than that in the US. The social discourse that was used in the US by rBGH critics has a long and deep history in Europe, and that, I would argue, played an important part in shaping the ultimate European Union decision not to permit the commercialization of rBGH.

In the EU context, this social discourse is closely wedded to the history of the social welfare state. State social welfare provision amounts to recognition that the market and private mechanisms cannot solve all social and economic problems. As a consequence, it is often appropriate for the state to intervene on the basis of implicitly agreed social values. By and large, in Europe, while this discourse probably has roots in the late nineteenth century, its development is primarily a product of the post-Second World War period.

One can see this discourse at work in the statements of any number of European Union politicians. Thus, for example, one Dutch member of the European Parliament echoed the concerns of many of others in the Parliament, when he argued that "The use of the BST hormone does increase unfair competition and social inequality, both between producers and between regions" (European Parliament 1988a: 17). Along similar lines, a parliamentary report expressed concern about the "long-term socioeconomic effects, particularly on the smaller farm," of the commercialization of rBGH in Europe (European Parliament 1988b).

It is safe to say that the power of this discourse made it possible for EU politicians to articulate a policy for evaluating technology that would theoretically prohibit the development of certain technologies if they did not meet the social goals of the Union. It was legitimate, indeed reasonable, to explicitly assert that not all economic problems can be resolved in or by the market. It allowed opponents of rBGH to be taken seriously when they asserted, against a form of technological progressivism, that ostensibly technical criteria commonly used to assess veterinary medicines provided an insufficient basis for evaluating rBGH and that a new technology was not automatically good or beneficial.

In December of 1999, after over a decade of debate and study by EU politicians and civil servants and after several temporary moratoria, the European Council of the European Union established a permanent ban on the commercial use of recombinant bovine growth hormone (rBGH) in European Union countries. In the end, the primary justification for the ban was not the likely social impacts of rBGH. Instead, pressure from the World Trade Organization and the need for compromise among EU policy-makers led to prohibition based on the likely health effects for dairy cows. This said, throughout the decade of discussion, social criteria of assessment figured centrally and were used to justify several temporary moratoria. Thus, although the existence of a social discourse cannot alone explain the EU rBGH policy debate, it did play a significant part (see Kleinman & Kinchy 2003a and 2003b).

In this section of chapter 2, I have considered policy debates over the appropriate path for the development of agricultural biotechnology. My point in highlighting these episodes is to suggest that in addition to the factors discussed earlier – the historically established structure of the agricultural sector and corporate power – that shape technological development and who benefits from new technologies, the discursive terrain also matters. The taken for granted understandings that people have about science, technology, and the market affect what they believe are appropriate technology development practices and policies, and dominant cultural understandings surely affect the decisions elected officials and civil servants make.

CONCLUSIONS

In this chapter, I have sought to provide a critical analysis of some of the early developments in agricultural biotechnology. Unlike a good deal of the analysis on this topic, I have not explored the possible human health effects of these emerging technologies or their conceivable environmental impacts. These are important topics, but they have received a fair bit of coverage elsewhere. Instead, I focused on the social processes that explain the particular trajectory of development of agricultural biotechnology, especially in the United States. I have argued that to understand the technologies that have been developed and to grasp their likely social implications one needs to understand the historically established structure of the agricultural sector and the social organization of power within it. By and large, the path of development that agricultural biotechnology has followed has been shaped by agribusiness in ways consistent with developments since at least the Second World War. Beyond agribusiness, the beneficiaries of these developments are likely to be large-scale producers whose farm organization and orientation is consistent with historical trends. Smaller producers who seek, for example, to produce for organic markets are likely to face ongoing struggles.

In showing that the particular path along which agricultural biotechnology has developed is not somehow intrinsic to the technology itself, I have posed an empirical challenge to technological progressivism. But in presenting an argument that points to a particular configuration of social forces as defining the road of development, I do not intend to replace technological determinism with a kind of social determinism. A technological progressivist argument suggests that it is the technology itself that automatically propels development down a singular path. I do not mean to say instead that social forces inevitably push development down an inescapable road. Trajectories of technological development are substantially the product of social struggles, and the existing organization of societies and the distribution of power within them notwithstanding, contingencies do sometimes produce unexpected outcomes. Subordinate participants in such struggles always have a chance to shape history, and drawing on historically resonant but often underutilized discourses can sometimes – as in the case of rBGH in the EU – alter outcomes. I do contend, however, that the existing organization of society – by shaping the relative power of actors and the extent to which particular technological choices appear legitimate and appropriate – does increase the likelihood that a particular direction of development will be followed.

NOTES

1   While farmers received some 21 percent of the income generated by the US agricultural economy in 1910, by 1990 their share was only 5 percent (Lacy 2000).
2   Beyond the socioeconomic effects on which I focus here, herbicide-tolerant crops may have environmental impacts as well. Because less care is required in using HRCs (because the crops themselves are protected from herbicide damage), herbicide use my accelerate, and this in turn may increase the rate at which weeds develop resistance to glyphosate-based herbicides. Farmers who use Roundup Ready soybeans are applying as much as five times the amount of herbicides as farmers using other methods of weed control, and the use of glyphosate has doubled since 1996 and the introduction of GM varieties (Kloppenburg 2004).
3   Versions of this section and the next appear in Kleinman and Kinchy (2003a and 2003b).

3

Rethinking Information Technology: Caught in the World Wide Web

According to many analysts, we are in the midst of an information revolution. Information technology is one of the two cornerstones of our new postindustrial economy. Today, the use of computers is commonplace in homes, workplaces, and schools; many people in this country "surf" the World Wide Web regularly. And given our fetishization of technology, it is perhaps not surprising that the bursting of the information-technology investment bubble in recent years has not led to increased public skepticism about what the technology has to offer. According to a 2003 *New York Times* article, "consumers, rather than paring back, are increasingly turning to all sorts of digital gadgets and services – cameras, music players, videodisc players, advanced television sets, cellphones, instant messaging, email, online shopping, high-speed internet access" (Lohr 2003: A1, C4).

While there may be somewhat more skepticism about the virtues of information technology than there was several years ago, there is a widespread sense that this "revolutionary" phenomenon will be the solution to an array of problems – some of which we have yet to become aware of. Information technology will, according to advocates: increase industrial productivity, facilitate tourism, improve the delivery of social services, allow educational services to reach out of the way places, improve government accountability, provide needed data to isolated farmers, foster a worldwide civic society, and mobilize social movements. But these cyber-optimistic predictions skate over a complicated reality. In this chapter, I hope to capture some of that complexity by stressing that to understand the possibilities for these new information technologies we must be attentive to the world into which they enter. In particular, I explore three dimensions of the revolution in information technology. First, I consider the so-called digital divide in computer and internet access. Here, I provide an analysis of the ways in which computer and information access are stratified across different social groups and regions. Next, I analyze the use of information technology in education. And finally, I consider what information technology means and is likely to mean for politics and civic life.

UNDERSTANDING THE DIGITAL DIVIDE

With a report in 1995, the Clinton administration first expressed its concern that there was a divide between those with access to information technology and those who lack it (US Department of Commerce 1995). Introducing subsequent reports, administration officials found the digital divide alarming because, they asserted, information tools and skills are crucial to full participation in the digitally driven economy (US Department of Commerce 1999; US Department of Commerce 2000). In other words, benefiting from the economic prosperity that has been and will be brought by the information technology revolution demands that individuals have access to the tools and skills that are the foundation of this economy.

What is the nature of the current digital divide? In terms of income, as of 2000, under 20 percent of households with income below $15,000 annually had computers and just about 13 percent of individuals with income below $15,000 had internet access. By contrast, nearly half of middle-income ($35,000 to $49,999) households and individuals had computers and internet access. Some 86 percent of households with incomes above $75,000 had computers, and nearly 80 percent of individuals with income above $75,000 had internet access (Servon 2002: 5).

The new high speed internet access technologies are not yet widely utilized, but already there is an income-based divide. According to Castells, nearly 14 percent of the most affluent online households in the US have broadband access. By contrast, under 8 percent of the poorest group do (2001: 256). This may prove to be among the most important dimensions of the digital divide because speed and bandwidth are, according to Castells, "essential for fulfilling the promise of the internet. All projected services and applications that people will really need for their work and lives," says Castells, "depend on access to these new transmission technologies. Thus, it could well happen that while the huddled masses finally have access to the phone-line internet, the global elites will have already escaped into a higher circle of cyberspace" (Castells 2001: 256).

In terms of race, according to data from 2000, just over 50 percent of Whites in the US had internet access, while about 30 percent of Blacks and under a quarter of Latinos did. And this gap is not only a reflection of income differences across race. That is, it is not just poor people of color who lack access to information technologies. Indeed, holding income constant only erases half of the difference between Whites and Blacks (Castells 2001: 251, 252).

While there was evidence by 2001 that the gap between Blacks and Whites in terms of internet access had begun to close, what this means is complicated. According to recent research completed on behalf of the Pew Foundation, "Blacks still do not have the same level and kind of access to the internet as Whites." Furthermore, Blacks with internet access do not go online as often as Whites, and a smaller percentage of Blacks with internet access send email on a given day than Whites (Servon 2002: 31).

Should we be surprised that there are disparities in access to and use of new information technologies? After all, we live in a highly stratified society. Indeed, one might argue that the digital divide simply reflects other more deeply entrenched dimensions of socioeconomic stratification. The gap between the rich and poor in the US is large, and in recent years it has been growing. According to one source, "Between 1979 and 1999, the average after-tax income of the wealthiest one percent of households went up 119.7%. The bottom fifth of households lost 12% and the middle fifth lost 3.1%" (Collins & Yeskel 2000: 39). According to that same source, "the top 1 percent of income-earners, 2.7 million people receive 50.4% of the national income, more than the poorest 100 million people" (Collins & Yeskel 2000: 39). In 2000, the average income of the wealthiest 400 American taxpayers was $173.9 million, whereas in 2001, median household income in the US was just $42,228. Average household income was slightly higher at $58,208, but the bottom 20 percent of all households had income between zero and just under $18,000 (OMB Watch 2003). Census data suggest that at the turn of the twenty-first century over 12 percent of all Americans were in poverty. The poverty line for 2001 was just over $9,000 for individuals and just over $18,000 for a family of four (www.census.gov/hhes/www/poverty.html; accessed 10/31/04).

There are substantial gaps between Whites and people of color as well. The percentage of Blacks and Latinos below the poverty threshold is nearly twice that for Whites, and the median income of Blacks and Latinos is under 50 percent of that of Whites. In addition to these disparities there are significant gaps within minority populations. Thus, for example, the income of the lowest fifth of Black income earners fell by just below 10 percent between 1979 and 1997, while the income of wealthiest 20 percent of Black income earners grew by 21.4 percent and the wealthiest 5 percent saw their income go up by over 30 percent during that same period (Collins & Yeskel 2000: 43). Until the mid-1960s, race played a larger role than class in determining the occupation and income achievements of Blacks. Starting in this period, "prosperous Blacks began to move ahead and low-income Blacks began to move backwards" (Collins & Yeskel 2000: 45).

Inequality in the US is of long standing, and there is no reason to believe that improving access to information technology will improve the situation (Servon 2002: 7). According to one analyst, "gaps in education, income, and occupation remain substantial and show no signs of closure during the first decade" after the commercial introduction of the internet (Norris 2001: 235).

Indeed, the digital divide in the US reflects deeply entrenched structural sources of inequality (Norris 2001: 16).[1] A thorough explanation for inequality is beyond the scope of this book, but I can make a few points. First, the organization of capitalist societies advantages those who are already well-placed along various socioeconomic matrices. Thus, for example, children from wealthy families are more likely to go to college than students from poor families. And a college degree is likely to create occupational and economic opportunities for these people. Even more important in explaining the life station in which one finds oneself may be one's parents's occupation, income and education (Jencks et al. 1972). Opportunities for upward mobility are systematically lower for people from families with lower income and educational attainment (MacLeod 1995). Beyond these deeply structural factors, the rise in inequality in recent years reflects, at least in part, public policies – tax, trade, and other economic policies – that have favored the asset rich at the expense of asset poor wage earners (Collins & Yeskel 2000: 68).

If the US picture seems bleak, the extent of inequality in the US pales when we make comparison across countries. Half of the world's 6 billion people live on less than 2 dollars a day (Collins & Yeskel 2000: 61). As of 1998, the world's 225 richest people had a combined annual income equivalent to the world's 2.5 billion poorest people (Collins & Yeskel 2000: 61). It should come as little surprise then that about 87 percent of people online live in postindustrial societies (Norris 2001: 15). Over 50 percent of people in the US surf the web, whereas only 0.1 percent of Nigerians do (Norris 2001: 15). As in the US case, the digital divide between the first and third worlds reflects deeper structural inequalities. According to Norris, "the evidence strongly suggests that economic development is the main factor driving access to digital technologies, so that the internet reflects and reinforces traditional inequalities between rich and poor societies" (Norris 2001: 15). And decades of research shows that uneven and inadequate economic development in countries in the southern hemisphere can be attributed in part to the economic domination of that region by industrial powers like the United States (Chew & Denmark 1996).

Policies to improve access to computers and the internet may close the gap between the digital haves and have-nots, but without attention by policy-makers to the deeper roots of inequality, the information technology revolution is more likely to help the already advantaged than to improve economic opportunity within the US.[2] Beyond the US, as Norris's research shows, in the internet's first decade "the availability of the internet has ... reinforced existing economic inequalities, rather than overcoming or transforming them." "The reasons," according to Norris, "are that levels of economic development combined with investments in research and development go a long way toward explaining those countries at the forefront of the internet revolution and those lagging far, far behind" (Norris 2001: 66, 67).

HIGH-TECHNOLOGY EDUCATION

Information technology in primary and secondary schools

In this section, I explore the increasing usage of information technology in all education environments. I focus the bulk of my attention on primary and secondary education, but consider higher education as well.

Driven by something that looks a lot like technological progressivism and, in particular, the idea that new technology is invariably better and means progress, educators and education administrators for all levels of schooling have jumped on the information technology bandwagon. Computers are found in classrooms from preschool through secondary school; ownership of laptop computers is required of students at some universities, and the first stop for entering university students is the information services office where they are allocated an email address.

It seems fair to say that the current approach to computer and internet use in primary and secondary schools reflects the deeply entrenched character of schooling in the US and current trends in education. To begin with, use of information technology reflects the widespread commitment to strict accountability systems, competency-based education, systems management, formalization, and testing in education circles. As of the late 1990s, nearly 40 of 50 US states had programs of statewide competency testing (Apple & Jungck 1998: 136). While the purpose of such exams, as is regularly noted, "is ostensibly to guarantee some form of 'quality control,' one of the major effects of such state intervention has been to put considerable pressure on teachers to teach simply for the tests" (Apple & Jungck 1998: 136). As a result, according to Servon, "Rather than using IT as a tool to foster creative thinking and problem solving, many schools have employed it as another way to do rote work such as math and spelling drills." Not surprisingly, applications like these have not produced impressive results (Servon 2002: 112; see also Bromley 1998: 15). Indeed, for the primary grades at least, there is little evidence that computer usage is associated with improved learning (Cordes & Miller 2000: 19).

Beyond arguing for the integration of computer technology into existing curricula, some proponents of information technology in primary and secondary education argue that facility with information technology itself must be taught. According to Servon, possession of IT skills is crucial for success in later life and work (2002: 108). However, basic computer use skills – typing and word processing, spreadsheet use, web search skills – can be taught to older students in very little time. There is no need to teach them early on, and focus on such skills inevitably means students are missing something else. Moreover, with rapid changes in the character of computer hardware and software over relatively short periods, teaching children specific computer skills early on may be setting them up for failure, as these skills may be obsolete by the time the children reach the adult job market. Teaching analytic, problem-solving, and literary skills and promoting creativity are more likely, in my view, to lead to success on the job market than teaching specific, concrete computer skills. In this context, one teacher interviewed by Servon said: "I would make the case that if you are just teaching technical knowledge to kids that are in school, then maybe you are doing that at the expense of giving them an education . . . If you give them the tools for learning then when HTML is gone they are going to master the next generation after that" (Servon 2002: 115). Warschauer makes a different but related point. He suggests that reading, writing, and thinking skills are required to use information technology effectively (2003: 109).

Evidence that fundamental analytical and learning skills, rather than basic computer skills, are what should be taught to children is made clear in a list of skills that students at New Techology High School in Napa, California, must master before graduation. They are: collaboration, problem-solving, oral communication, written communication, career building, technological literacy, citizenship and ethics, and content literacy (Servon 2002: 116). Technology and content literacy are specifically related to information technology. The other skills are not. Indeed, a look at a wide range of programs aimed at bridging the digital divide through education makes clear that even those who push IT-oriented education implicitly recognize that the crucial tools students need are not related specifically to the technology. Programs stress such general orientations as following a project through from start to finish and teaching children to work in small groups (Servon 2002: 122ff.). Children are socialized to the work world in some programs (Servon 2002: 128), and through developing products using IT, students are likely to develop "self-confidence, determination, teamwork, [and] problem-solving" (Servon 2002: 132); these are general orientations that are important independent of computer technology and the IT revolution.

Lisa Servon is an advocate of teaching IT skills to children. However, it is not clear that her own work supports the importance of teaching them computer-specific skills. Indeed, while Servon gushes about the technical skills children learn in the programs she studies – for example, webpage design – she does not make a compelling case for the importance of teaching low-income children such narrow and time sensitive skills. The nature of such skills is likely to change substantially by the time kids enter the world of work, and in learning fundamentals, children are more likely to be well-positioned to succeed than by learning easily taught skills that are likely to be outdated by the time children seek career employment.

Although in her work Servon stresses the importance of high-quality IT training in allowing young people and workers to get ahead economically, the nature of the courses she views as successful (2002: 137) and the level of technological proficiency for the occupations she discusses (2002: 151) do not seem to support this. Instead, the courses focus on basic skill development (e.g. analytic skills), and in the occupations she highlights, the actual technical proficiency required is fairly low. The precise technical skills can be attained in a relatively short period of time (from 3 months to 2 years). In addition, probably recognizing the site-specific character of skills as well as the rapid change in required technical knowledge, firms are increasingly recognizing the importance of in-house training, as against teaching IT skills in school (Servon 2002: 159).

While it might be possible to thoroughly integrate information technology into existing curricula – to use these tools creatively – and not just for rote exercises or developing facility with the technology itself, the current fiscal climate means examples of such usage are few and far between.[3] Schools are understaffed and teachers are undertrained in the use of computers. According to Apple and Jungck, the teachers they followed did not have time to give students individual assistance in computer usage (1998: 148). Moreover, "lack of comprehensive curriculum-planning time is characteristic of the structure of most schools" (1998: 152), and teachers and administrators, according to one analyst, "have not been taught to think about how to integrate technology into what they do" (Servon 2002: 111). Finally, schools are spending much less time on training than most analysts say is necessary (Cordes & Miller 2000: 78). In this context, according to one report, teachers need 3 to 6 years to learn how to effectively integrate computers into their classrooms (Cordes & Miller 2000: 79). However, in the US, a 1997 study sponsored by the US Department of Education found that most teachers had not been trained to use information technology in their teaching, and just 15 percent indicated that they had had at least 9 hours of relevant training (cited in Castells 2001: 258). Now, the spread of information technology has increased significantly since the mid-1990s; however, a survey undertaken by the National Center for Educational Statistics found that only 20 percent of "teachers feel prepared to integrate IT into their classrooms" (cited in Servon 2002: 111).

I have shown that the concern with standardization, a commitment to preparing students for the world of work and fiscal crises are shaping the use of computer technology in primary and secondary schools. But in addition, there are what we might term "opportunity costs" to the use of computers in classrooms across the United States. On the financial side, the decision to use our scarce dollars in one way means that they cannot be used in another. According to one estimate, "US public schools have spent more than $27 billion on computer technology and related expenses" in only 5 years in the middle 1990s, and yearly spending on information technology for schools "has more than doubled since the 1994–1995 school year, rising from about $3.6 billion that year to an estimated $7.8 billion for 1999–2000" (Cordes & Miller 2000: 77).

Beyond the budgetary tradeoffs, there are time tradeoffs as well. The more time students spend on computers, the less time they will have to spend interacting with fellow students and with teachers (Cordes & Miller 2000: 30). One might argue that such interaction is crucial for the development of skills necessary to work successfully in groups – an important capacity in the current economy – and for the development of commitments to community and good citizenship. According to one source, some research suggests that building student–teacher bonds and a strong sense of community in schools can improve educational performance (Cordes & Miller 2000: 30), and heavy reliance on IT in schools is likely to weaken student–teacher interaction and time for community building.

Basic analytic skills, interactive capacities, and negotiating abilities all have longer shelf lives than basic computer skills, and this brings me to a final issue of import for primary and secondary school students: the class character of American education. Historically, at least, students preparing for working-class jobs were essentially trained to be disciplined in their work practice and to follow orders (Bowles & Gintis 1976). Those destined for white-collar employment were more likely to learn general analytical and leadership skills. The new economy blurs the lines between the kinds of skills required of managers and workers, but it seems more likely that children from more affluent backgrounds will be able to escape the regimented character of American education than will children from less affluent backgrounds. When it comes to information technology, children from less affluent backgrounds are more likely to use computers for remedial drills, and to learn how to run specific computer programs and perhaps how to build websites, while children from more affluent backgrounds are more likely to "learn to learn" – to develop the skills "to decide what to look for, how to retrieve it, how to process it, and how to use it for the specific task that prompted the search for information" on the web (Castells 2001: 259; Warschauer 2003: 116, 131). If this occurs, then access to information technology in the schools will serve only to reinforce widespread social stratification, not to undermine it.

Universities, computers, and the internet

Like public elementary and secondary schools, public universities are confronting a fiscal crisis, and administrators and faculty members are expected to do more with less. This crisis of resources has in many ways served as an impetus for the introduction of information technologies to higher education. But beyond what we might term factors of the moment, not surprisingly, the deeper logic of higher education has shaped the introduction of these new tools as well.

Online education is a sensible reaction to fiscal belt-tightening. Commercial entities can be persuaded to invest in such initiatives, and advocates believe that the per student cost of such efforts can permit budget trimming. As David Noble notes, "The foremost promoters of [online education] . . . are . . . the vendors of the network hardware, software, and 'content' – Apple, IBM, Bell, the cable companies, Microsoft, and the edutainment and publishing companies Disney, Simon and Schuster, Prentice-Hall, et al. – who view education as a market for their wares, a market estimated by the Lehman Brothers investment firm to be potentially worth several hundred billion dollars" (Noble 2001: 29). In short, unlike what happens in a traditional university classroom, the infrastructure and content for online education can be bought and sold. It can be made into a commodity.

The crucial question is: does online education offer the same quality as face-to-face higher education? At one level, this new educational mode mirrors and reinforces the approach to teaching one finds in large lecture classes in universities throughout the country. Students are largely passive and the professor conveys information from the front of the room, where s/he is invested with the authority that comes with knowledge (Bromley 1998: 23). Such an approach does not allow for the idea that students are not only knowledge recipients, but knowledge producers. It is inattentive to the idea that mastery of information demands interaction. To do more than ingest information, students must interact with faculty members as well as with fellow students. In this context, it is perhaps not surprising that dropout rates for online distance education are much higher than those for students enrolled in classroom-based programs (Noble 2001: 23).

It is surely the case that to make education available to a wide array of students, large lectures and even online education may be necessary; however, true education is labor intensive and depends on low student–teacher ratios (Noble 2001: 4). Higher education in the US, like so much else, is stratified. Those who can afford to often go to smaller private institutions where they are more likely than those who must go to public institutions to have easy access to faculty members. Online education initiatives are likely to reinforce this reality.

More generally, we should ask if schooling – higher education, in particular – is about *education* or *training*. As David Noble notes, *training* is about "honing of a person's mind so that . . . [it] can be used for the purposes of someone other than that person" (2001: 2). By contrast, *education* aims to promote the integration of knowledge, critical analytical skills, and, for Noble, self-knowledge through bringing together knowledge and self. Online education is likely to reinforce trends toward training students. Education will be available to fewer and fewer students.

In general, I expect that a stronger case for integrating information technology into real university classroom environments can be made than for online education. Professors can use electronic mail to prompt discussion outside of classroom hours and can develop websites with links to sources faculty members want their students to have access to. On the other hand, I have come across too many students in recent years who have never been to the university library and have no idea how to access the array of resources available there, and those students who turn exclusively to the internet as the source for their research material typically have no idea how to assess the material they find. Indeed, as Warschauer suggests, in the internet age, the ability of students to critically assess their information sources may be more important than it was when students relied on published sources. Warschauer notes that books are vetted twice: once by publishers and once by the librarians who purchase them. Without such vetting, it is more important than ever that students learn to evaluate the credibility and viewpoint of the sources on which they draw (2003: 114).

Finally, and beyond the effects on students, the move to online education has had and will continue to have effects on faculty members. As Noble suggests, the spread of computer technology and online courses in higher education is likely to reduce the control faculty have over their work products and their time. Universities and the commercial entities with which they contract are likely to own the lectures and materials prepared by faculty (Noble 2002). This could make well-trained faculty increasingly disposable. In addition, the use of electronic mail and chatrooms is likely to extend and intensify the working time of faculty, as students increasingly expect their professors to be available at all times of day and night and expect near instantaneous responses to their requests and queries. In addition, of course, where faculty members attempt to integrate online content into their real-time courses, the time spent in developing this material is time that they do not have to spend directly with students.

POLITICS, CIVIC ACTION, AND THE INTERNET

Most of those who consider the place for the internet in politics and organizing for social change contend that the internet will strengthen democracy, by expanding possibilities for accountability of policy-makers and
reducing the economic and other costs for political participation (Norris
2001: 96ff., 112; Boyd 2003). A more pessimistic forecast would expect
politics of/on the internet to reflect and reinforce the existing character of
governmental decision-making and electoral politics. My own sense is that
generally the internet seems to mean more politics as usual, but that the
technology has created some opportunities for making political action in a
different way than it has generally been made and that this should give us
tempered hope. In this section, I review developments in the use of the internet by government agencies, elected officials, political parties and non-
governmental organizations.

In the area of what we might call e-governance, analysis of the content
of government websites throughout the world shows that websites tend to
be used by government agencies as mechanisms for posting information
rather than to promote greater interaction between government and citizens (Norris 2001: 122). A study of parliamentary websites across the globe
indicates that these cyberspaces are used primarily to provide contact information, biographical materials about elected officials, schedules, history,
draft legislation and other government documents (Norris 2001: 139).
According to Castells, insofar as such sites have an interactive component,
assistants to members of parliament (presumably including members of the
US Congress), tend to respond to citizen requests in the same way they used
to respond to written letters (2001: 155; see also Norris 2001: 114). While
these sites then do not constitute a profound change in governance, the
provision of government information via the internet may broaden the
population of those who have access to government information and thus
weaken government control of information, thereby improving government
transparency and accountability (Norris 2001: 122, 123; Warschauer 2003:
172–81). That said, a report sponsored by the Organization for Economic
Cooperation and Development from the mid-1990s found that "the internet has failed to increase access to policy-makers, to improve the transparency of government decisionmaking, or to facilitate public participation
in policy making" (cited in Norris 2001: 113, 114).

If we turn our attention to the websites of political parties, we find a
decidedly mixed bag. On the one hand, a systemic comparison of party
websites worldwide found little evidence that these sites are providing an
opportunity for substantial "bottom-up" feedback (Norris 2001: 150). On
the other hand, as Norris suggests, although political parties are likely to

provide information on their websites that they believe is most likely to attract members, "Insofar as much of this information is often not readily available from other sources, and as long as the public can compare information across competing websites, this process can be seen to add to electoral competition in representative democracy" (Norris 2001: 169).

In terms of the economic capacity that major versus minor parties have to use the web and to create websites, parties with greater financial resources are likely to be better able to create and maintain professionally developed websites (Norris 2001: 156). At the same time, Norris's analysis of political parties across the globe from minor to major suggests that although the web does not level the political playing field for parties, it does "provide a more egalitarian environment where technical expertise counts in gathering information and communicating messages" (Norris 2001: 239).

In the US, politicians are beginning to use the internet more seriously for electoral purposes. Early evidence points to the advantage gained by insurgent campaigns that are among the first to utilize the internet to build support and an organization. Democratic presidential candidate Howard Dean used software that facilitates bringing possible supporters together. These efforts prompted widespread enthusiasm for the campaign and brought in substantial campaign revenue. In mid-August of 2003, Dean appeared on the cover of both *Time* and *Newsweek*. He rose quickly from being a dark horse to being the candidate to beat. Because the costs of this campaigning approach are lower than sending individual political organizers to strategic locales, insurgent campaigns may benefit from this technology. On the other hand, it is not clear that without traditional organizing vehicles a candidate can win nationwide office, let alone local office. Lack of a well-developed grassroots structure may have hurt Dean. Moreover, the early advantage Dean gained may have resulted from his being an early adopter of a new technology. As more established campaigns increasingly deploy the internet along with traditional campaign strategies and resources, the early adopter and leveling advantages may be lost. This appears to have been the case in the 2004 presidential contest. In Dean's case, simply drawing untargeted support from throughout the country was not enough to capture the Democratic nomination (Boyd 2003: 17).

The greatest opportunity to remake politics may come from social movements's use of the internet. As Norris notes, flash movements – movements prompted by particular events or issues, like the antiglobalization protests in Seattle – suggest that the internet "has the capacity to alter the structure of opportunities for communication and information in civic society. In this environment a culture is provided that is particularly conducive for alternative social movements, fringe parties . . . seeking to organize and mobilize dispersed groups for collective action" (Norris 2001: 191).

In this context, Boyd notes that the internet "allows large mobilizations to unfold with minimal bureaucracy and hierarchy" (Boyd 2003: 13; see also Warschauer 2003: 191–7). In February of 2003, the internet was used to organize peace demonstrations globally (Boyd 2003). That initiative brought people from all over the world together at specific locations in a call for peace. Some 400,000 people gathered in New York City. A month later, MoveOn, an organization with 5 paid staffers, using a 1.5 million person mailing list and software called "the meeting tool," was able to facilitate the mobilization of "an estimated 1 million people in more than 6,000 gatherings in 130 countries and every state in the nation" (Boyd 2003: 14). The organizing costs of this effort were very low, and MoveOn raised millions of dollars online to run antiwar advertisements on TV and in print. The organization gathered one million signatures on a petition for the United Nations Security Council and coordinated 200,000 phone calls to elected officials in Washington DC on a single day (Boyd 2003: 14).

In terms of the potential to deepen democracy and increase citizen input in shaping policy and civic life in general, such cases are, in my view, heartening. Still, surveys of online users and the general public suggest that "People who used the e-political resources available on the internet were drawn from the population that was already among the most motivated, informed, and interested in the American electorate" (cited in Norris 2001: 218). Indeed, Norris wonders "whether the internet can ever encourage the less engaged to take advantage of these opportunities at a mass level . . . because as the medium of choice par excellence, it becomes even easier for people to tune out from public life" (2001: 24). So it is not clear that internet tools are drawing in the previously disenfranchised, and because organizations like MoveOn set the threshold for political participation so low (Katz & Rice 2002: 330), it is not clear that these organizations are really creating new activists. Finally, insofar as such initiatives substitute for permanent, structured, and formal movement organizations, their ultimate efficacy is open to question (Castells 2001: 141).

Cass Sunstein (2001) worries that the internet revolution could impoverish civic life at a deeper level. He contends that the internet has the potential to allow citizens to filter what they see and hear in a way that was not possible in the pre-internet days.[4] But democracy, he argues, demands that we be exposed to information and ideas that we did not search out, did not intend to see. Such exposure reduces the chances of extremism – a situation made all too easy when people only confront the views with which they already agree and only interact with people who share those views. Such exposure also reduces the likelihood of political fragmentation. Increasing fragmentation, according to Bimber, will mean less interest-group politics and more issue-based politics with less institutional coherence (cited in Norris 2001: 174). In addition, Sunstein believes that widespread use of the internet could reduce the number of common experiences shared by citizens. Such experiences, Sunstein contends, make it possible for people in a diverse society to understand one another and work together to solve social problems.

At a time when civic engagement is, by some measures, at an all-time low, Sunstein's concerns seem worth contemplating, but these are not new problems. Indeed, Sunstein acknowledges that the internet may simply reinforce the tendency of citizens to filter their information. Thus, again, we find that the technology reflects and reinforces the way our social order is organized. Building a strong civic and political life is not as much about technology, as it is about working to create the underlying mechanisms to make deep democracy work.

CONCLUSIONS

Proponents of computers and the internet tell us that the revolution in information technology will bring us a new world. Instead, in this chapter, I have argued that developments in information technology reflect the social world in which we *already* live. Why should we have expected an equitable, much less equal, distribution of computer technology and internet access, when none of the more basic resources in our society is allocated in that fashion? Income, wealth, and access to quality primary, secondary, and tertiary education are all very unevenly distributed in the US today. What is more, there is little reason to believe that equalizing access to information technology will be the solution to all of society's ills – most particularly poverty. Indeed, the assorted forms of inequality that we face are of long standing. If we cannot mitigate the social advantages that those born to well-educated and higher income families begin with, if we cannot find ways to weaken deeply institutionalized racism, offering a computer in every home and a high speed portal in every room will very likely do little to make the US the meritocracy it aspires to be. Indeed, if we are not able to address these deeper problems, the revolution in information technology is likely to reinforce the advantages already possessed by those Americans who are socioeconomically well-situated. Outside the US, in the countries of the southern hemisphere, there is equally little reason to believe the computer revolution will replace poverty with paradise. More fundamental questions about industrial infrastructure and balanced economies must be addressed before spreading computers and the internet will make much of a difference.

In classrooms too, optimists – technological progressivists – imagine that computers and the internet will fix a system of education that is widely acknowledged to be broken. But in ways that have a shorter history than widespread socioeconomic inequality, the uses to which computer technology in education are being put in the US reflect existing educational policy and fiscal constraints. The computerization of primary and secondary education reflects increased standardization and formalization, and, thus, creative uses of these tools are often overlooked in favor of the routine and mundane. In the face of budget shortfalls, computers can become babysitters for students, and many teachers acknowledge their training is not up to the task of using computers in an innovative and agile manner. Furthermore, a careful look suggests that what is being taught in programs that claim to teach students to work with information technology is, at least as importantly, fundamental skills, and it may be that our system of education would move further toward preparing students for successful and satisfying work and civic lives by focusing on these essential skills. Finally, in the matter of distance education at the university level, one can imagine that for some students this development will create real opportunities, but we should not overlook the fact that this approach reflects a very traditional pedagogy and is likely to be one case where the digital divide is reversed: those from less advantaged backgrounds, if they received a university education at all, will increasingly receive it – whether on campus or off – at some distance from their teachers, who, working with large numbers of students, are not likely to have time for much one-on-one interaction. By contrast, more economically fortunate students will still have opportunities to attend institutions where small seminar classes are the order of the day and the honing of basic skills (reasoning, writing, speaking) is the aim.

Finally, there is the matter of information technology in politics and civic life. For the most part, the evidence does not point to innovative uses of this tool by those in the political establishment. Instead, computers and the internet are used to conduct business as usual. On the other hand, there is some evidence that the internet can enhance the organizing capacities of those outside the established order and bring a voice to the previously disenfranchised. But we should be cautious here. To begin with, there is no reason to believe that information technology will relieve the alienation of the socially disengaged. And the shallowness of commitment demanded by flash movements does not point to the internet as the basis for well-integrated and powerful social movements. Finally, well-resourced organizations will retain an advantage, as they will be able to create more sophisticated websites, regularly update them, and find ways to engage their grassroots.

The case of the development of information technology is at one level very similar to that of biotechnology in agriculture: both reflect the existing organization of society and much of the impetus behind them is a technological progressivist vision that sees new technology as inherently good and a solution to the problems we confront. But they are different too. The trajectory that agricultural biotechnology has taken reflects corporate domination of agriculture and the vision of agriculture promoted by the likes of Monsanto. Of course, computers and the internet are today developed and promoted by business interests too, and there is some reason to be concerned about the commercialization of computer-based education. However, the impacts of the information technology revolution reflect at once broader and more deeply entrenched structures – like the social stratification of societies – and more momentary phenomena – as in the case of the fiscal crisis facing American education.

NOTES

1   While I suggest that the digital divide "reflects" more basic forms of inequality, Warschauer makes the case that the relations between digital and other forms of inequality are mutually reinforcing (2003: 7).
2   Warschauer makes a slightly different, but important point: equal access to information technology does not imply equal ability to use the technology, which may depend on education and literacy, content and language, among other factors (2003: 58).
3   Warschauer describes some examples he believes are creative and salubrious instances of information technology use in primary and secondary education (2003: 135–8).
4   For a contrasting view, see Katz & Rice (2002: 332).

4

Owning Technoscience: Understanding the New Intellectual Property Battles

In the summer of 2003, I boarded a bus in Madison, Wisconsin, bound for Chicago. A young woman sitting in front of me was listening to a portable CD player. The music blared, loud enough that I could hear that it ran the gamut from Barry Manilow to Jimi Hendrix to some postpunk band. When she removed her CD from the player, I could see handwritten across the top the word "Favorites."

That same summer, I had the good fortune to travel to Aix-en-Provence, France. While there, I visited one of the city's most important cultural sites: Cézanne's studio. In the midst of a tour of the artist's working area one of my fellow tourists took a photo. He was sharply reprimanded and quickly offered to delete the image from his digital camera.

Several summers earlier, I was working in a university biology laboratory when discussion at a lab meeting turned to the possibility of manufacturing in-house a polymerase widely used in biological research. Researchers hoped to bring down the cost of the substance and to adapt it for the lab's specific uses.

At some level, these incidents need not reflect a particular era. When I was young my friends and I would compile our favorite songs on cassette tapes for concentrated listening. And I surely remember occasions at cultural sites during which a visitor was asked by an official not to take photographs. As for making research tools, scientists have manufactured these to their specifications in-house perhaps since the beginning of science as a modern practice. But each of the cases I described is emblematic of a new age in which at one and the same time the world is increasingly made up of protected intellectual property – copyright protected songs and patented inventions – and new technologies open a vast space for creativity and innovation.

Making a CD for one's private use from one's own music collection still falls within the legal category of "fair use," and if this is how the young woman I described made her CD she is well within her rights. If, on the other hand, she downloaded the music from an internet music site without making payment to copyright owners, she may have been guilty of infringement. The tourist in Aix was just doing what many of us have done, and the copyright status of his action has not changed in recent years, but his ability to immediately erase the photographic image (or for that matter to creatively alter it) is new. Finally, while a discussion in a university lab about in-house manufacture of research tools might have been heard 20, 50, or 75 years ago, the awareness of the leaders of the laboratory that in-house manufacture of the particular polymerase of interest might raise patent infringement considerations is new.

Commitment to intellectual property protection in the US is as old as the country itself. The first article of the United States Constitution says that "The Congress shall have Power . . . To promote the progress of science and the useful arts, by securing for limited times to authors and inventors the exclusive right to their respective writings and discoveries." The aim of such protection was to create an incentive to innovation. But in our new knowledge economy the net of intellectual property protection is vastly tighter than it was in earlier ages. At a time when new technologies enhance human creative possibilities, the increasingly broad reach of intellectual property protection threatens that same creative potential. And in this age when knowledge and information are the currency of progress and prosperity, matters of intellectual property are creating and reinforcing new social cleavages, empowering some and alienating and disempowering others.

This chapter explores the problem of intellectual property protection in our technoscientific age. I begin my discussion by exploring the social common sense about the value of intellectual property protection, and then provide a critique of these supposed virtues that we take for granted. Here, I argue for the crucial importance of a knowledge commons – a social space where ideas can be relatively freely drawn upon without the limits imposed by private-property rights in ideas – to collective economic prosperity and creative advancement. In the second half of the chapter, I discuss the issues of innovation promotion, equity, and social stratification raised by several recent technoscientific developments. This portion of the chapter deals first with digital technologies and later with developments in biology.

Before turning to the substance of this chapter, I need to provide readers with a bit of terminological background. Intellectual property can be defined as a work, idea, or invention that can be owned and protected by law. Of the three primary varieties of intellectual property law in the US – patent, copyright, and trademark – I will be concerned only about the first two. Patent law aims to encourage invention by granting a temporary monopoly (currently 20 years in the US) to an inventor of a tangible, useful, novel, and non-obvious device or process. A patent protects not only the ideas on which an invention is based but also the specific invention. Thus, a subsequent invention that is similar to an existing patented invention would be considered an infringement of the patent (Vaidhyanathan 2001: 18). Patents may be granted for new processes, machines, and "compositions of matter." Patents may also be granted for a design as a means of protecting new ways of planning or constructing articles of manufacture. Beyond these two types of patents, a distinct law provides protection for new varieties of plants (Kloppenburg 1988). In contrast to patents, copyright is supposed to provide protection for literary, artistic, and musical work. More recently, computer generated work has been added to the list of what is copyrightable. Originality is a central requirement for copyright protection. Like patent protection, copyright is supposed to provide creators with protection of their work for a limited period, but today that limited period amounts to the life of the author plus 70 years.

INTELLECTUAL PROPERTY, SOCIAL COMMON SENSE, AND THE KNOWLEDGE COMMONS

At a most basic level, in the United States we take the primacy of the individual for granted (see Bellah 1996; Kleinman 2003: 28ff.). Underlying our intellectual property regime is the idea that we are a society made up of individuals, rather than a collective entity that is somehow greater than the individuals that constitute it. This idea matters for intellectual property law because it leads us to assume that individual genius leads to creative invention. In this context specifically, we take for granted a nineteenth-century Romantic notion of authorship – that isolated autonomous individuals produce innovation (Boyle 1996). There is no recognition in this social common sense that all new ideas draw on old ones, and that, therefore, creativity and innovation depend fundamentally on a collectively produced sphere of ideas – a knowledge commons.

The second half of the discourse that shapes our collective views of intellectual property protection is that individual initiative, above all, leads to individual success (MacLeod 1995) and national economic well-being. But initiative, according to this logic, depends on some incentive to create; without incentive, creation would not occur. If individual genius explains innovation, but innovation demands an incentive, private-property rights are understood to be the basis of that incentive. That is, we assume the correctness of exchanging an invention for property rights to that invention. And we go further, imagining that that "progress always comes from dividing resources among private owners; that the more dividing we do, the better off we will be; that the free is an exception, or an imperfection, which depends upon altruism, or carelessness, or a commitment to communism" (Lessig 2001: 13). We take this line of reasoning so for granted that to call it reasoning is perhaps a misnomer. We accept the virtue of private property without limitation.

Given this social common sense, the trend in intellectual property law has been to progressively enlarge the kinds of ideas and objects that are protectable and to undervalue or ignore the importance of sources and audiences in the process of innovation. This failure to recognize the importance of the knowledge commons – that all ideas ultimately have their source in existing ideas (Vaidhyanathan 2001: 64, 65) or that "free content . . . is crucial to building and supporting new content" (ibid.: 50) – is clear in the cases that follow and in trends in intellectual property law more generally. The result, as I will argue in the conclusion of this chapter, is that we may be quickly losing a vibrant public domain, and without such a space "creativity is crippled" (Lessig 2001: 14).

INTELLECTUAL PROPERTY AND THE INFORMATION TECHNOLOGY REVOLUTION

In this section, I consider three cases in the history of innovation in information technology that illustrate the tension between property and the public domain, and how this tension serves to array unevenly matched sides in struggles to (re)define the intellectual property regime for the digital age. I begin with a discussion of rap music, and then move to consider user-to-user music sharing networks like Napster, and conclude with an analysis of computer software and intellectual property.

In rap music, "artists often 'sample' bits of others' melody and harmony, and use those 'samples' as part of a rhythm track, completely transforming and recycling those pieces of music" (Vaidhyanathan 2001: 131). In the early days of this musical form, young Black intercity rappers often used "piles of warped vinyl . . . [to create] scraps of sounds" (Vaidhyanathan 2001: 132). Interest in the musical form grew substantially over the years, climbing from 11.6 percent of the US music sales market in 1987 to 18.3 percent three years later (Vaidhyanathan 2001: 133).

Sampling became a contentious issue in the US music industry, as digital technology became affordable for many aspiring artists. As Siva Vaidhyanathan suggests, "Digital sampling . . . had a powerful democratizing effect on American popular music. All a young composer needed was a thick stack of vinyl albums, a $2,000 sampler, a microphone, and a tapedeck, and she could make fresh and powerful music" (2001: 138). From the perspective of a number of music critics and certainly rap performers, what rappers do with the samples they utilize is to create new sounds – new music. Siva Vaidhyanathan suggests that "The new, composite, mosaic work is assembled from these samples through an independent application of skill, labor, and judgment" (2001: 139). However, given the way in which samples are utilized, rap constitutes an explicit challenge to well-established notions in US copyright, raising questions like: What counts as novel "work"? Who is an "author"? And what is "originality" (Vaidhyanathan 2001: 139)? In raising these questions, this new musical form threatens large entertainment corporations and established musicians who contend that this new art form amounts to theft.

Many would argue that sampling is consistent with the concept of "fair use" which has historically been central to copyright protection. This is the idea, apiece with the view that a knowledge commons is central to ongoing creativity, that in the development of new creative work, creators can draw on a reasonable amount of already existing creative work. But in keeping with what I have described as the social common sense on intellectual property, those in a position to shape the intellectual property regime increasingly undervalue the knowledge commons, and thus, fair use has taken on an increasingly narrow meaning. In 1991, a US federal court judge ruled that the sampling of 20 seconds from an existing recording amounted to theft. According to Vaidhyanathan, this decision "all but shut down the practice of unauthorized sampling in rap music" (2001: 141). It left virtually no room for fair use, and as a result, since 1991, there has been a significant decrease in the amount of sampling in popular music. According to Vaidhyanathan, the 1991 decision "removed from rap music a whole level of communication and meaning that once played a part in the audience's reception to it" (2001: 143, 144).

And, indeed, the notion of fair use drawn on by the music industry and the courts is ultimately quite narrow. The US Federal courts's ruling on such matters and the recording industry have not seriously considered whether use of a sample in a new work weakens the market for the original song. In the case of rap music, had this standard been applied, sampling might well be legal today. Indeed, the amount of music sampled, combined with the substantial difference in style between rap music and the music typically sampled, means that the market for sampled work would rarely be undermined by sampling (Vaidhyanathan 2001: 144).

Why do I raise this issue in a book about science and technology, when after all the connection to technology may seem quite tenuous? The answer is twofold. First, and most directly relevant, although sampling started with analogue technology (record or LP turntables), digital technology brought rap music to an entirely new level, making possible a kind of musical blending that previously would not have been possible. It is certainly reasonable to conclude that without digital sampling technology, rap music would not have come to constitute such a threat to entertainment corporations and established entertainers. Second, this case illustrates clearly what is happening to the knowledge commons in our new knowledge economy. The nature of this sphere will surely shape the future of developments in science and technology in the years to come.

Beyond the factors that tie this case to the general theme of this book, rap music merits discussion because it clearly illustrates the kinds of social struggles that can emerge as the twenty-first century gets underway. Here we have a conflict between financially powerful corporations (and established musicians) and typically resource-weak artists. These artists are generally not in a position to challenge deep-pocketed corporations and musicians. Indeed, as Vaidhyanathan notes, "by the late 1990s, rap artists without the support of a major record company and its lawyers, without a large pool of money to pay license fees for samples, had a choice: either don't sample or don't market new music" (2001: 133; see also 137).

An especially important development in the information age is the rise of networks. Music sharing services draw on computer networks and deploy a compression technology known as MP3, which allows music to circulate on the internet simply and efficiently. The best-known service using MP3 technology is Napster. Developed by a college student named Sean Fanning, Napster was a "peer-to-peer" sound file trading system, which was released on the internet in August of 1999 (McCourt & Burkhart 2003: 338). According to McCourt and Burkhart, "Its brokered architecture effectively coordinated peers and increased search functionality, and its search and play interface was highly user-friendly" (2003: 339).

Vaidhyanathan calls Napster a public library for music (2001: 180). Needless to say, the recording industry did not view the service in that way. Instead, industry representatives saw Napster as equivalent to theft. In December of 1999, the Recording Industry Association of America, a group made up of all the major music labels, sued Napster essentially for music piracy, arguing that the service allowed people across the globe to share and copy music files for free. In July of 2000, the US Federal District Court ruled in the industry's favor, and in February of 2001, the US Federal Court of Appeals affirmed the lower court's ruling, effectively shutting Napster down (McCourt & Burkhart 2003: 339).

The Napster court decision notwithstanding, there is an argument to be made for systems like Napster, a case thoroughly consistent with the philosophy underlying US copyright law at its inception. First, Napster allows consumers to "taste" the music that interests them and makes available content to individual consumers. Listeners need not rely on disc jockeys (Lessig 2001: 132) or the record industry (McCourt & Burkhart 2003: 336). As Vaidhyanathan argues, services like Napster makes "music fans more informed consumers . . . MP3s let consumers taste before they buy"

(2001: 180, 181). Such systems empower consumers, in some cases linking them directly to artists (McCourt & Burkhart 2003: 336), and put pressure on the industry to be responsive to emerging consumer demands. While this would seem to advantage consumers vis-à-vis the industry, the industry could gain as well. With the MP3 technology "apparent 'trends' would not surprise companies in the future" (Vaidhyanathan 2001: 180, 181). Moreover, a 2000 survey suggests that permitting the free downloading of music may serve a marketing function. Sixty percent of respondents to this survey said that listening to a song online led later to a CD or cassette purchase (cited in McCourt & Burkhart 2003: 347n12). The industry is not opposed to electronic distribution, but they want to control distribution and set prices.

A second possible advantage of MP3 technology is that distribution through such systems potentially broadens the audience for the new work of emerging artists. New artists face higher barriers than established musicians in their efforts to attract listeners, and these artists are precisely the people copyright law was created to encourage. However, as Vaidhyanathan notes, "Because the established music industry narrows the pipes of production and distribution, manufacturing scarcity, only established artists profit from the old system" (Vaidhyanathan 2001: 180). A third possible advantage of MP3 technology is the access it offers to difficult-to-obtain music. A significant portion of the content offered by Napster is music that is no longer sold by the major recording labels. Distribution, using MP3 technology, provides widespread access to a range of music that prior to the spread of this technology was largely unavailable to consumers (Lessig 2001: 131). And while distribution of this material may at some level constitute competition for entertainment industry corporations, it does not really substitute for the demand served by the industry.

The Napster case clearly illustrates how an obsession with the virtues of private property and a failure to recognize the value of fair use and the knowledge commons can hurt consumers and emerging and faded artists alike. The development of MP3 technology within the context of our social common sense about intellectual property constructs social cleavages – divisions that ultimately benefit the well-established and powerful and hurt and disadvantage the less powerful.

Finally, in this section, I turn my attention to computer software and intellectual property issues. Software constitutes the instructions that, responding to a user, make our computers function. Underlying all software is source code: the "collection of logical languages designed to instruct the computer what it should do" (Lessig 2001: 50). Early developments in software resulted from collaboration between universities, the federal government, and industry. And during the early days, the culture of software developments reflected a commitment to openness and sharing (Saxenian

1994). Researchers from academia as well as industry and government commonly made their source code available to other researchers. Into the 1970s, software firms regularly made source code available with their software. This allowed programmers to improve and customize purchased software. But as Siva Vaidhyanathan tells the story, "once the industry outgrew its own incubators, a different, conflicting value infected its practices. What was once public, shared, collaborative, and experimental became secret, proprietary, and jealously guarded" (2001: 154).

By the 1980s, companies increasingly kept source code secret, recognizing that doing so had commercial value. For software users, this was clearly a troubling development. Programmers outside manufacturing companies could no longer build on existing software, eliminating glitches and making improvements. Instead, they were dependent on software companies to produce the particular software features that they needed and wanted. What had been part of the knowledge commons and had allowed the industry to develop and thrive began to close (Vaidhyanathan 2001: 154).

A development that was particularly troubling to programmers was the decision of AT&T to retain the source code for the UNIX operating system. An operating system might be viewed as the master software for a computer. It tells a computer how to use its resources, interacting with the application-specific software that users deploy to undertake various tasks from word processing to surfing the World Wide Web. UNIX is a common and powerful operating system first available in the 1980s. It was a product of university–corporate collaboration, but distributed by AT&T. Given the collaborative nature of its development, computer programmers were angered by the company's decision to withhold the source code from users. To these professionals, AT&T's action violated an open culture of long standing.

Although there is clearly a general trend to proprietize all manner of information technology, those opposed to such trends are not always helpless in the face of this movement. In the UNIX case, programmers did not take the discourse of property and individual initiative for granted. Instead, they worked in a culture with an alternative, if subordinate at a society-wide level, discourse. And unlike rap artists or Napster users, they had a resources – a capacity or power – that enabled them to respond to the enclosure movement in which AT&T and other companies were engaged. They were in a position to develop alternative software, and given this ability, they could enforce a cultural alternative to the standard intellectual property regime.

When AT&T declined to release the source code for UNIX, nobody was more outraged than Richard Stallman. At the time a computer scientist at Massachusetts Institute of Technology working on artificial intelligence, Stallman left the Institute in 1984 and founded the Free Software

Foundation in 1985, thus initiating the free software movement. This movement was premised on four essential freedoms: to run a program for any purpose, to study how a program works and adapt it, to redistribute copies of any program, and to improve any program and release these improvements for public use (www.gnu.org/philosophy/free-sw.html; accessed Nov. 30, 2004; Lessig 2001: 53).[1]

Other advocates of free software and open source code developed LINUX – an open source alternative to UNIX – in the 1990s. They faced the problem, however, that if open source advocates were to release programs using LINUX, but not copyright them, large computer companies might put a stranglehold on these programs by simply adding a limited number of features that they protected via copyright. Stallman developed a strategy for subverting any effort to enclose the software commons. He outlined a licensing practice he termed "copyleft." This idea requires that people who copy or change Free Software agree to publicly release any changes to that software, and any future license made on any changes must follow copyleft principles. Thus, as Vaidhyanathan stresses, "the license perpetuates itself. It spreads the principle of openness and sharing wherever someone chooses to use it" (Vaidhyanathan 2001: 156).

Today, Linux is a widely used operating system, although it has not displaced UNIX. It is even used in the "mainstream" computer industry (Vaidhyanathan 2001: 156). But while the free software movement and copyleft constitute a clear alternative to the taken-for-granted intellectual property discourse, they have not fundamentally displaced that discourse or the practices associated with it. Indeed, Vaidhyanathan views the free software orientation as ultimately "fringe" within the software industry (2001: 156).

Owning Life: Intellectual Property in Biological Materials

Although not always realized in practice, like early software research, biological research developed in an environment with an explicit commitment to common property in research materials. But a broad commitment to sharing in the name of scientific advance has been largely displaced by a commitment to private property associated with the development of the biotechnology industry. The filing of a patent for the basic procedure used in recombinant DNA procedures marks the starting point of this trend. But if this technical innovation and the action taken by its developers and their universities was a crucial factor in the trend toward patenting in the biological sciences, several judicial and administrative decisions were also important. First in 1980, the US Supreme Court ruled in the case of *Diamond v. Chakrabarty* that living organisms were patentable. The micro-organism at issue in this case was the product of recombinant DNA (rDNA) techniques and the court ruled that it was not, therefore, a product of nature (such substances were viewed, at the time, as unpatentable), but reflected creativity, initiative, and imagination. The organism was engineered to "eat" oil and thus might serve as a tool in cleaning up oil spills. As a result, this life form was not only a human creation, but also useful. It was, thus, patentable. From micro-organisms, court decisions were arrived at that permitted patenting of plants and animals of all kinds. In 1985, the *Chakrabarty* decision was broadened, when the US Patent and Trademark Board of Appeals determined that, in principle, any type of plant could be patented. Two years later, the Patent and Trademark Office ruled that all living animals could, in theory, be protected as intellectual property through patenting. These developments and related policy determinations have fundamentally altered the practice of biological science and even, to a degree, medicine (see Kleinman 2003).

In the biological sciences, we can see the enclosure of the knowledge commons in several recent cases related to research tools. The first instance involves a polymerase used in the amplification of DNA (see Kleinman 2003). The polymerase is known as *Taq*. *Taq* is an enzyme that comes from the bacteria *Thermus aquaticus*, an organism that was originally found in a thermal pool in Yellowstone National Park. *Taq* plays a crucial role in increasing the efficiency of DNA amplification because, since it survives repeated heating and cooling, it need not be replaced during every round of amplification. The controversy around *Taq* centers on Promega, a biotechnology company, and Hoffmann–La Roche, a multinational healthcare giant. But the dispute has implications broadly for the knowledge commons and specifically for academic scientists.

Hoffmann–La Roche obtained the patent for *Taq* from another biotechnology company called Cetus in 1991. At the time of this transaction, Promega had a license to manufacture and sell *Taq*. But the license permitted Promega to sell *Taq* as a generic enzyme; the company was not supposed to sell the substance for use in the amplification of DNA. Believing Promega was doing just that, La Roche sued. As part of its lawsuit and clearly in an effort to improve its bottom line by monopolizing sales of *Taq*, in the spring of 1995, Hoffmann–La Roche named 40 universities and government laboratories in the US as well as 200 academic researchers who the company claimed were violating their patent by purchasing *Taq* from Promega and then using it in the process of amplifying DNA.

The lawsuit has not been resolved at this writing, and La Roche claims that it has no intention of pursuing legal action against academic researchers. Still, in principle, the position taken by the company amounts to a direct and explicit challenge to what is known as the "experimental use exemption" (Heller & Eisenberg 1998).[2] Not formally enshrined in law, but adhered to in practice, this "tradition" allows researchers who are not engaged in research with commercial aims – scientists undertaking what is commonly called fundamental or basic research – to use patented materials for research purposes without explicit permission or formal license. The experimental use exemption makes possible – although it does not guarantee – the flexible and unencumbered exchange of research materials. The narrowing of this exemption could threaten the flow of what might be broadly termed research knowledge and thus slow the innovation process. Beyond this, the action of Hoffmann–La Roche pits unevenly matched interests against one another. Academic researchers could theoretically continue to purchase *Taq* from Promega and then use it in DNA amplification, or they might even manufacture the enzyme themselves in their own laboratories. However, either action could put these scientists at risk of lawsuit. And while academic scientists may have morality as well as common-law tradition on their side, Hoffmann–La Roche has trends in intellectual property law, our social common sense, and, perhaps most importantly, money on its side. Most academic researchers – like new rap artists in their relationship to the recording industry – simply lack the economic wherewithal to challenge La Roche's action.

At about the same time the *Taq* controversy was unfolding, a case raising similar issues was developing around a technology called Cre-*lox*P (see Kleinman 2003). Developed by scientists employed by the DuPont Corporation, a multinational chemical concern, this technology allows researchers to manipulate genes in mice. With Cre-*lox*P, scientists can design mice to meet their research needs. With a 1990 patent on the technology, DuPont is in a position to regulate how this important research tools is used – even in noncommercial cases – and the company requires any scientist who uses Cre-*lox*P mice to acknowledge the company's rights to the animals. Additionally, DuPont demands that researchers who use their technology and subsequently make discoveries that are profitable with it, pay the company a share of profits. Most crucially, researchers who do not agree to DuPont's terms are forbidden from using this important research tool.

DuPont's requirements for use of the technology developed in its laboratories generally constitute a barrier to the free flow of research materials and information among scientists. These restrictions amount to a narrowing of the knowledge commons. The possible paperwork burden alone is likely to slow research, and the financial considerations, in particular any fee for use of Cre-*lox*P, could constitute a barrier to research in academic laboratories facing government budget crises.

Like the *Taq* case, the Cre-*lox*P episode raises questions of a power imbalance between researchers and companies (Kleinman 2003). Here, the company controls a powerful research tool, and it may decline to provide it to researchers who do not agree to its terms. And while researchers might stress the experimental use exemption tradition as the basis for allowing Cre-*lox*P mice to flow freely among university researchers, these scientists typically will not have the capacity to enforce their desires. As in the *Taq* case, the company has trends in intellectual property law and social common sense on its side, and the economic capacity to enforce its will in the courts.

A final instance involving research tools, and worthy of discussion, directly affects relations *between* academic scientists. In the late 1990s universities began to use "material transfer agreements." According to academic tradition – although again not always in reality (Kleinman 2003) – researchers who publish work that describes a research material are expected to provide that material upon request to other researchers. University administrators, recognizing the commercial potential of the materials developed by their scientists, have begun to require that before they offer their materials to other researchers these other researchers be required to sign a material transfer agreement. These contracts can narrow the knowledge commons by demanding restrictions on publication in exchange for the desired research material. Often delays in publication are desired by universities so that they can clarify intellectual property rights before results are made public.

Although this case does not pit academic scientists against multinational corporations, it does pit scientists against much more economically powerful entities than they, entities that have the capacity to restrict the flow of research materials and to take legal action against scientists who violate material transfer agreements. Furthermore, as in the *Taq* and the Cre-*lox*P cases, because a given university may be the only source of a crucial research material, academic scientists may have no alternative but to agree to contract terms that restrict their freedom of movement and thus narrow the knowledge commons.

One final case related to biological research is worthy of mention. This episode involved Raul Cano, a molecular biologist and a founder of Ambergene Corporation. In 1995, Cano reported successfully having extracted the genetic material from ancient micro-organisms encased in amber (see Shulman 1999: 9). There was widespread concern among scientists that what Cano asserted to be ancient DNA was in fact DNA from contemporary organisms that had contaminated Cano's samples. Debate about the quality of experimental protocols in science is not uncommon (Collins & Pinch 1993), and generally in such cases, other scientists will make an effort to replicate the disputed experiment to see if they can reproduce the questioned results. In this case, however, Cano received a patent on the technique he used to extract the genetic material from amber. As a result, Cano can prevent scientists formally from interrogating his results, and, insofar as his techniques are sound, Cano can prevent researchers from making related attempts to recover genetic material from amber. Cano has, in effect, used patent law to narrow the knowledge commons in two ways.

Outside academic laboratories, the strangling grip of intellectual property restrictions are increasingly felt in the medical arena. As in the culture of research, medical doctors have come to expect that techniques developed by colleagues will be freely available to them in the interest of helping their patients. Indeed, according to the former president of the American Medical Association, the Hippocratic Oath requires that doctors share information with their colleagues (Shulman 1999: 35). In keeping, however, with trends to make ideas into commodities, by the mid-1990s, the US Patent and Trademark Office was granting some 100 patents monthly on medical procedures. Thus, in 1993, one eye surgeon was sued for patent infringement for a "no-stitch" technique for removing cataracts. Other physicians have received letters demanding royalties for using a patented technique for determining the sex of a fetus at 12 to 14 weeks using ultrasound. And doctors have claimed patent rights for techniques such as making slits in a skin graft to expand it and suturing the stomach to the intestines. In many such cases, these techniques were in widespread use before patents were granted or royalties demanded. Some, like the ultrasound gender-determining technique, are viewed by physicians as obvious. However, according to Seth Shulman, "because patent examiners, who are seldom medical practitioners themselves, base their decisions on searches of published work that often poorly reflect the unfolding state of medical knowledge, patents are frequently granted for procedures that are not particularly novel or even noteworthy" (1999: 36). At one level, then, many of these patents could be viewed as errors and may ultimately be determined to be invalid, but the efforts to obtain them in the first place points to the ever-spreading belief in the virtue of proprietizing anything and everything with little recognition of the possible social costs. Physicians's access to critical techniques could be limited, and they may become leery of sharing their own experiences with colleagues (Shulman 1999: 36, 37). Furthermore, patenting of medical techniques raises the possibility of increasing the cost of medical care, and this would obviously affect the uninsured and lower-income patients disproportionately.

The no-stitch cataract surgery case came to the attention of a member of Congress who was also a physician. In a time of the rapid spread of the commodification of ideas, Representative Greg Ganske argued that the idea of patenting medical procedures simply contradicted the social role of medicine. He proposed legislation to prohibit the patenting of such techniques. As with much in American policy-making, the final legislation reflected compromise. The final law, signed by President Bill Clinton in 1996, responds to the worries of the biotechnology industry that their innovations be protected and to the concerns of the medical community. The law allows for patents on medical procedures, but frees doctors from liability where they use patented techniques in their practices (Shulman 1999: 41, 42). In the end, this law is a rather narrow exception to developing trends, and the law does not apply retroactively. Thus, doctors can still be sued for infringing any medical procedure patent granted before the act's passage. Here, as in the case of rap artists sampling under the authority of "fair use" and researchers using techniques and materials on the ground of the "experimental use exemption," doctors without the financial capacity to defend themselves in court will not be able to challenge clear violations of the culture of medicine and, indeed, may not be able to use techniques patented prior to the Act's passage if they cannot afford to pay required licensing fees.

As I discuss in more detail in the next chapter, intellectual property disputes are not restricted to struggles between interests within the United States. They can also pit US- and Europe-based corporations, and a US government serving the interests of such corporations, against the people and countries of the southern hemisphere. Among the most recent of such clashes is that between manufacturers of AIDS drugs and the countries and peoples of South Africa, who have been hit particularly hard by the AIDS pandemic.

Some 5,500 people are killed by AIDS daily in Sub-Saharan Africa (Castellblanch 2000). In 2000, there were an estimated 3.6 million HIV-positive South Africans (Hilton 2000). The life expectancy in South Africa is declining and is likely to drop further. Estimates suggest that absent AIDS, South Africans could expect to live on average to be 70 years of age by 2010; however, in the face of AIDS that estimate has been reduced to 50 (Castellblanch 2000). According to one source, "at least 30,000 South African children a year would not contract HIV from their mothers if HIV-positive pregnant women were treated with the antiviral drug zidovudine (AZT). But the exorbitant cost of this drug is preventing infected women from getting treatment" (Castellblanch 2000). In this relatively poor country, the price of drugs effective in the fight against AIDS is exactly the problem. In 2000, Glaxo Wellcome was charging US$240 a month for AZT in South Africa (Castellblanch 2000). Put differently, the cost of treating an individual with AIDS each month was almost 8 times the average household income in South Africa (Hilton 2000). And one estimate puts the cost of "antiretroviral cocktails" in Africa in the late-1990s much higher, at $10,000 per person annually (McNeil 2001). Drugs developed to fight AIDS were intended initially for the western market – a set of countries of considerably greater wealth than South Africa and other countries in the southern hemisphere – and with well-developed medical infrastructures. The drugs are protected intellectual property, and drug companies with a monopoly on them price their products on that basis.

Initially, drug companies did little more than provide relatively meager donations of needed drugs to South Africa. With little improvement in the availability of AIDS drugs, the government of South Africa passed the Medicines Act in 1997. This law allowed the government to secure AIDS and other drugs at a more modest cost, using two techniques consistent with international trade agreements. First, the government could establish compulsory licenses. Such licenses would require drug companies holding patents on AIDS drugs to license them to manufacturers specified by the government. Second, through a practice known as parallel importing, the government can allow companies to buy drugs from another country, where prices are cheaper, and resell them in South Africa (Castellblanch 2000).

The Medicines Act poses a substantial threat to the intellectual property rights of multinational drug concerns. Soon after its passage, the industry filed suit in South African court, challenging the law. At the time, the industry had an ally in the US government, which put pressure on South Africa by publicly asserting that the country was not a safe place in which to invest (Hilton 2000; Castellblanch 2000). While the suit was tied up in court, the 39 involved drug companies closed their South African factories, canceled investments, and repeatedly asserted that the South African government wanted to undermine the system of intellectual property protection (Swarns 2001).

In reaction, "an unlikely coalition" of AIDS activists, doctors from Europe, and African officials and lawyers undertook an array of protest actions, effectively conveying the sense, through the international media, that "poor Africans . . . were dying because they lacked AIDS drugs" (Swarns 2001: A6). In addition, the US government changed its position, quietly adding pressure to the activists' cause, and the European Union, the World Health Organization, and other national and international bodies came out in support of the South African government's position in the lawsuit (Swarns 2001). Ultimately, in an outcome out of step with current trends in intellectual protection, in 2001, the companies involved dropped their claim (Pollack 2001). Perhaps fearing the precedent that would be set if the South African government permitted patented drugs to be manufactured against the will of patent-holding companies by firms that produce generic drugs, the major drug companies decided to sell their drugs substantially below their former price in the South African market. At the time of the drug companies' move, only about 10,000 South Africans were receiving the AIDS drugs they needed. That number was expected to jump ten-fold within a year of their agreeing to work with the South African government to make drugs available more cheaply (Swarns 2001).

In accepting defeat, the drug companies have not conceded the need to rethink intellectual property protection. Indeed, their settlement in this case notwithstanding, the involved companies continue to argue that patenting is essential to promote innovation and that drug development will slow to a trickle without such legal backing (Pollack 2001). But given the levels of poverty in Africa, the likelihood that these companies will commit to the development of, for example, drugs to fight tropical diseases is small. Indeed, the action of these companies was narrowly strategic. By conceding the moral appropriateness of making high priced drugs available to poor people in this single case, they have made no general acknowledgment that intellectual property protection has limitations. While a subsequent international agreement concedes the need to limit patent enforcement in the face of health crises (Kahn 2001), cases like this one clearly illustrate another way in which intellectual property reinforces a socially stratified world. In such cases, patent holders can often use their patents to enforce prices that effectively deny access to innovation to the poor. On occasion, social movements may challenge the trend of ever-widening intellectual property protection, but they are unlikely to stop it, and these cases should lead us to ask about the social virtues of intellectual property protection.

INTELLECTUAL PROPERTY AND INNOVATION

The cases I have just discussed concerning medical techniques and medicine raise very real questions about consumer access to vital resources in the face of intellectual property protection and about what it means to have intellectual property in a world divided between rich and poor, powerful and weak. Beyond these issues, throughout the chapter, I have focused on the ways intellectual property protection pits large corporations against relatively poor and weak prospective innovators. This conflict speaks to a broader question about the efficacy of intellectual property protection. Proponents of the progressive bolstering of the US and international intellectual property protection regime argue that patent and copyright protection are important mechanisms for the promotion of innovation, and without such protection innovation would slow substantially. In this section, I want to provide a more systematic challenge to this position.

Corporate representatives in technoscientific fields regularly assert the centrality of patent protection to promote innovation (Kleinman 2003: 131, 132). This assertion has become the social common sense, and this "faith" in the causal link between patenting and innovation "guides people's action" (Samuelson 1987: 12). Decisively showing the import and efficacy of patent protection would be difficult because we do not have a developed (post)industrial national economy in which intellectual property is not protected with which to compare, for example, the United States and ascertain whether there are different levels of innovation in the two economies. That said, with the exception of pharmaceuticals (Lessig 2001: 206), there is virtually no positive evidence that the patent system promotes widespread innovation and the broad use of inventions (Dworkin 1987), and there is data to suggest the overall effects of expansive patent protection are "small and often negative" (Benkler 2004: 1110). Positive evidence indicates that there are times and industries where patent protection does not promote innovation. Research suggests, for example, that patenting activity in the semiconductor industry is not associated with innovation (cited in Lessig 2001: 206). More generally, economists have found that in cases where it is not clear specifically how an innovation can be drawn on in a new product, licensing of a patent is unlikely. Thus, the invention is not likely to be used, and the patent may have served only to restrict the use of the innovation (Lessig 2001: 205). Additionally, where companies devote their time and energy to acquiring and defending patents, their practices may lead to less attention to innovation than might otherwise occur (Lessig 2001: 206). Related to this, "multiple and overlapping patent protection may create an anticommons, where innovators are afraid to innovate in a field because too many people have the right to veto the use of a particular resource or idea" (Lessig 2001: 215).[3]

On the copyright front, the breadth of legal protection has, as I have noted, extended rather substantially over the past more than 200 years. Certainly, the case can be made that prior to the lengthening of the copyright term as a result of the 1998 Sony Bono Term Extension Act, substantial innovation occurred. Over the centuries and in particular in recent years, "The balance of copyright law has moved away from promoting creative liberty and toward the protection of 'property rights'" (Vaidhyanathan 2001: 11). As I have suggested, this shift has led to increasing restrictions in the flow of information, with incalculable negative effects on innovation. Copyright law initially established to promote stylistic innovation no longer serves that function. Importantly, in this context, the push behind the extension of copyright came primarily from corporate interests (McCourt & Burkhart 2003: 337). The extent to which the extended copyright term enters into the calculations of individual artists is doubtful. Surely, an artist will assess whether she can make a living creating art, but it is hard to imagine an artist making a thorough calculation about whether to write another book or make another CD based on the extent of copyright protection and, in particular, whether her estate will receive royalties many years after her death.

CONCLUSIONS

In this chapter, I have explored recent developments in intellectual property protection. I began by unpacking and critiquing our "social common sense" about intellectual property protection. Then I explored recent trends – first related information technology and then associated with biological innovations – that are narrowing the knowledge commons, reinforcing the power of already dominant social actors, and weakening the positions of subordinate actors.

Our social common sense has led us to progressively narrow the knowledge commons without evidence that doing so will increase our social well-being. Indeed, there is some evidence to suggest that the increasing breadth of coverage of intellectual property law is having or will have adverse affects on our broad social welfare.

The progressive closing of the knowledge commons typically pits the resource rich against the resource poor. In the biological sciences, threats of lawsuit by multinational companies holding patents to essential tools or products may constrain the research of university biologists and so innovation. In computer technology, research may be similarly constrained. In addition, however, legal threats from entertainment industry companies may limit the cultural resources on which emerging but unestablished artists can draw, making us all culturally poorer, and consumers may be barred from information that would allow them to make informed decisions about the music to which they want to listen and the films they want to see. Ironically, this limit could hurt the corporate producers of entertainment by suppressing market demand. Finally, in the case of crucial resources – like drugs and medical techniques – patent protection will serve to limit access to the world's rich citizens, raising profound moral questions.

NOTES

1 A somewhat similar initiative with regard to agriculture-related patents is called Public Intellectual Property for Agriculture (PIPRA). This initiative – a collaboration among agricultural research universities – promotes sharing university-produced intellectual property related to subsistence agriculture and specialty crop development (Benkler 2004; Kloppenburg 2004: ch. 11).

2 A subsequent court decision (in *Madley v. Duke University*) puts the right of an exemption to patent law for research purposes in doubt (Benkler 2004: 1111).

3 Although I focus on the downside of widespread patenting and the related narrowing of the knowledge commons, one reviewer of a draft of this book suggested that a move toward a less pervasive culture of patenting could result in an increase in trade secrets (intellectual property held in confidence and never

revealed to competitors). This outcome could certainly inhibit innovation, as building on existing inventions could become near impossible. By contrast, however, advocates of enlarging the knowledge commons suggest inventors and society at large could benefit if knowledge about innovations flowed more freely than it does today. Inventors would quickly build on existing inventions, leading to an increase in the speed of innovation, and profits would be generated not by holding a monopoly on an invention but, for example, by being first to market with a new commodity, through marketing, and early adopter advantages.

5

Technoscience in the Third World: The Politics of Indigenous Resources

Since the mid-1980s, dozens of patents have been issued to companies from the US and Japan for the use of "neem" in a range of products that draw on the plant's antibacterial properties. Neem is a tree native to India, and its medicinal and pesticidal qualities have been known in that country for hundreds of years. In India, neem has been used to fight tooth decay and agricultural pests, and indeed, according to one source, traditional knowledge in India is what inspired research in the global north to develop commodifiable neem-related products (Shiva 1997: 69–72). Another analyst suggests that even when the properties of neem had been studied in modern Indian laboratories, because the "Indian scientific-industrial nexus" is not well-developed, Indian companies have not been able to collect the information necessary to submit applications for all of the patents that, by any reasonable equity criteria, should stay in India (Philip 2001: 13). Under these circumstances, how do we value the traditional knowledge on which use of neem has been based for hundreds of years? Is this knowledge "scientific"? Whether or not it counts as science, does such knowledge make invalid any effort to patent neem-based products on the basis of their novelty? If products of neem are deemed patentable, should not Indians receive compensation for the knowledge and the plant that made these patents and potential profit possible?

At the heart of any understanding of technoscience in the global south (what some call the third world or developing countries) is the relationship between divergent understandings of knowledge and property in relationship to structures of power. Looking at the neem case, we need to ask what is valid knowledge? What is useful knowledge, and, in the end, what is science? Similarly, when we consider technoscientific developments arising out of the global south we are forced to ask: who owns a given technoscientific product and who owns a particular piece of knowledge? Answering these questions demands that we interrogate ideas about knowledge, science, and property largely taken for granted in the global north, and how these sometimes collide with quite divergent ideas that exist in specific locations and times in the global south. All of this must be understood in terms of a history of colonial and postcolonial relations between northern and southern countries and regions and how these histories shape the nature of power in the present day.

This chapter is organized into three sections. In the first, I investigate the relationship between colonialism and genetic resources. Here, I consider the centrality of genetic resources to the development of the economic infrastructures of colonial powers, exploring European imperial expansion and the neocolonial practices of the US. Among other issues, I contend with the divergent views of knowledge and property that are woven through this colonial history. This first section of the chapter lays the foundation for the second half of the chapter, which looks at recent developments in what might be termed biocolonialism. Recent economic and technological developments have made the global south a crucial site for resources of use in agriculture and medicine. In this section, I consider how colonial history laid the foundations for current relations and practices. More generally, I interrogate these contemporary relations and practices. Finally, I discuss three instances where some effort has been made to correct historical inequities in north – south relations around biological resources.

Science, Technology, and Colonialism

My empirical focus in this chapter is on biological resources and the knowledge related to them. In principle, any living thing can be a biological resource. Here, I focus on plants, microbes, and, to a lesser extent, animals, and the genetic material out of which they are constituted.

As fate would have it, the bulk of the world's genetic diversity – the wide-ranging genetic material that constitutes all living things – comes from the global south. All major food crops – those crops consumed and grown by most of the planet's population – originate in the tropics and subtropics (Kloppenburg & Kleinman 1988). Most domesticated animals have their "centers of origin" in the south as well. North America (that is, the current US and Canada), by contrast, has no indigenous mammalian livestock species, and no major crop plants are indigenous to North America. The diversity of species found in the oceans is also richest in the tropics, and tropical rainforests contain at least half of all known plant and animal species (Rural Advancement Foundation International 1997: 8).

Plants were collected and traded for use as food, drugs, and insecticides for millennia before the voyages of European exploration and the associated colonization. There is evidence that thousands of years before the Common Era, hundreds of plants or their extracts were used as drugs in China and Egypt (Merson 2001: 285). But the spread and value of exchange of plants changed with the voyages of exploration sponsored by European nations. When Columbus returned from his 1492 voyage, he brought with him not only news of new lands and peoples, but seeds of the maize plant (Kloppenburg 1988: 155). According to one source, "it was rare that any ship to or from the New World – or anywhere outside of Europe in the Age of Exploration – did not have a person knowledgeable about plants and potentially capable of exploiting their medicinal properties" (Dorsey 2001: 272). Other students of what might be called biocolonialism tell us that the king of Spain sent his personal physician to live with the Aztecs and study their medicine early in the mid-sixteenth century (Schultes & Reis, cited in Dorsey 2001: 272). The king was clearly interested not only in the biological materials found by Aztec peoples, but also in their knowledge of how to use these biologicals medicinally.

The so-called New World was not only the source of hugely important food, medicinal, and industrial crops, like cocoa, quinine, tobacco, sisal, and rubber, but also constituted "a new arena for the production of the Old World's plant commodities" (Kloppenburg 1988: 154). In addition, early voyages of exploration and related efforts of colonization initiated a complex web of exchanges. Thus, fewer than 50 years after crops from the Americas made their way to Europe, they could also be found in China. Mooney (1983: 85) describes a "botanical chess game" in which imperial initiatives brought crops like coffee from Ethiopia to the Caribbean, South and Central America, east Asia, southeast Asia, and east Africa for plantation production. Tea from China was transported to east Africa, and sugar cane from southeast Asia was scattered throughout colonial territories in the southern hemisphere (Kloppenburg 1988: 155).

These exchanges occurred over a long period and were associated with a complex colonial infrastructure. Thus, sugarcane was first transferred from southeast Asia to Syria and Egypt by Arab traders and farmers. The Venetians learned from Arabs the cultivation of sugarcane and its production through a slave-based plantation system. By the fourteenth century, the Venetians had displaced the Arabs in this production system. By the mid-seventeenth century, sugar and the slave trade were firmly entrenched in Barbados. As for coffee, according to one source, one plant from Java transferred to the Amsterdam Botanic Garden in 1706 is the source for the coffee initially grown in most New World plantations (Brockway 1988: 53).

Today, we think of our visits to botanical gardens in major urban centers as offering a wonderful reprieve from traffic jams and the sooty belching of power plants and factories. But these centers, built to house the genetic diversity found mostly in the global south, were a crucial tool in European empire-building. These institutions were used to adapt plants of economic and medicinal value from around the world for cultivation, and, according to Brockway, they "played a critical role in generating and disseminating useful scientific knowledge which facilitated transfers of energy, manpower, and capital on a worldwide basis and on an unprecedented scale" (1988: 49). According to one source, "imperial powers sought to control the cultivation of useful plants, with colonial botanical gardens providing crucial testing grounds for the suitability of plants to new climates" (Gillbank quoted in Merson 2001: 286). Importantly, the success of this botanical work depended crucially on the development of a systemized plant identification method, which was developed in the mid-eighteenth century by Carolus Linnaeus (Dorsey 2001: 272).

Perhaps the most famous botanical garden – the Royal Botanic Gardens at Kew in London, England – was run by eminent British scientists who served a crucial role in shaping the flow of knowledge about plant materials from imperial Britain to that nation's colonies and from colonial regions back to Britain. The case of cinchona seeds and saplings is characteristic. Cinchona was a crucial tool in imperial expansion, as its bark was the only known source for the treatment of malaria, a devastating disease in the southern hemisphere.

These plant materials were taken in the 1850s from the Peruvian Andes by an employee of the East India Company, a crucial institution in the expansion of British empire. Cinchona was grown and bred at Kew and then transplanted in south India. According to one source, the East India Company employee, Clements Markham, unambiguously and knowingly defied Peruvian law in taking plant materials. Markham claimed his appropriation of cinchona plants would benefit the peoples of the global south, but in the event, the quinine distilled from the plant's bark was distributed widely to British troops, but only available in very limited quantities to people from the Indian subcontinent (see Philip 2001: 8–10).

The history of rubber is also intimately tied to colonialism and Kew. In 1876, an employee of Kew took some 70,000 rubber tree seeds from Brazil. Sprouted at Kew, the resulting seedlings were taken to a botanic garden in Ceylon and then to another in Singapore. Although virtually all rubber came from Brazil up through the nineteenth century, by the First World War there was no rubber industry in that country, and by 1930 three-quarters of all rubber production came from British-owned plantations (Brockway 1988). Thus, colonial relations could serve to facilitate the industrial infrastructure and capacity of the already powerful countries from the northern hemisphere, while leaving southern hemisphere countries, with little in the way of developed industrial systems, to sell unrefined raw materials.

During the extended colonial era, expeditions for, and research on novel plant varieties provided a crucial basis for colonial advancement. The plant scientists affiliated with botanical gardens, like Kew, were not only engaging in the expansion of human knowledge of the world's flora, but played a crucial role in colonial expansion. The resources of the global south were often taken without permission through subterfuge or unambiguous theft. In this context, it is crucial to note again that the vast bulk of the world's genetic diversity comes from regions of the world that became the colonial territories of European nations, and that without the genetic wealth of these regions, colonial expansion would not have been possible. Still, European powers typically dismissed the idea that peoples of the global south might have any property rights to the genetic resources found in their lands (Merson 2001: 287).

The early history of the United States is marked by similar colonial-botanic practices. The only crops indigenous to the US are the sunflower, blueberry, cranberry, Jerusalem artichoke, and the pecan. Thus, the collection of food as well as industrial crop seed was crucial to the development of the United States. In 1819, the US Secretary of the Treasury required all consular and naval officers to collect potentially useful seeds and plants while abroad. The military too was expected to collect useful genetic material, and indeed, Admiral Perry returned from Japan with rice, soybean, vegetable, and citrus seeds and cuttings. Fully one-third of the US Department of Agriculture's budget at this time was to be expended on germplasm collection, and this practice continued well into the twentieth century, when the government sponsored regular expeditions throughout the world in search of new useful plant types (see Kloppenburg & Kleinman 1987).

In addition to the global search for plant genetic resources to bolster US agriculture, the Department of Agriculture as well as early agribusinesses scoured the globe for insects that could be used to control pests destructive of American agriculture. In the early twentieth century, Sunkist and other citrus cooperatives funded a trip by a scientist to South America in search of parasites to control a citrus scale (Sawyer 1996: 130). To ensure that the scientist, Harold Compere, was unencumbered in his investigation, he traveled as an agent of the US government, looking not only for protection against California red scale, but also for insects to combat other pests. Scientists from university entomology departments also traveled the globe in search of parasites that might control pests that threatened domestic agriculture (Sawyer 2001).

The use and development of biological materials from colonial regions intensified during the nineteenth century in Europe as well. At that time, "the application of the experimental methods of science to the extraction of active agents from biological material played a crucial role in establishing the chemical industry" (Merson 2001: 287). Biological extracts were pivotal in the colonies too. Quinine was first extracted in 1819, and, as I noted above, it played a crucial role in fighting malaria in colonial territories.

By the end of the nineteenth century, colonial powers had established institutes for the study of tropical diseases, and "The documentation of local medical practices, and the use of native plant material, soon became part of the process of fighting disease" (Merson 2001: 287). Colonial researchers learned the value of plants in the global south from observing their use by local peoples. Systematic exploration and careful observation led to medical cures for diseases that afflicted local people and colonists, but, in addition, Europeans engaged in crossbreeding of agricultural animals to develop hearty stock and simultaneously veterinary medicine.

There are several observations we might draw from this early history. First, the colonial politics of genetic resources played a crucial role in creating an asymmetry of economic and political power between the regions of the global north and south in what would ultimately become an integrated capitalist world system. Northern nations used the resources of the south to develop a system of northern agriculture that could sustain fully industrialized nations. Genetic materials from the south also led to developments in northern medicine. Second, this era of northern appropriation of genetic resources from the south laid the foundation for subsequent failures to recognize the genetic resources from the south as materials of value for which the peoples of the south merited compensation. In short, a boundary was created and reinforced between natural free resources and property. Finally, and relatedly, during the extended colonial period, a hierarchy of knowledge forms was implicitly developed and reinforced. While colonial agents learned from peoples of the global south about the biological resources found in their lands, the knowledge conveyed by southern peoples, like the diverse biological materials from the southern hemisphere, were not recognized or compensated for. Implicitly and explicitly, the biologically-related knowledge viewed as valuable for colonial expansion and industrial development came from the scientists, in particular those associated with botanical gardens, of the north. The implication of this asymmetry in recognition was that knowledge from the south was not knowledge at all, and certainly lacked the value of the scientific knowledge from the north.

To say that northern countries benefited disproportionately from the colonial exchange of biological materials is not to say that the era of exploration and subsequent colonialization affected residents within the colonizing countries and the colonized evenly. There is no question that not all Europeans benefited equally from that region's unambiguous exploitation of the global south, and certainly, those residents of colonized lands who created alliance with European colonial regimes likely benefited more from

European empire building than did poor peasants. Still, from a regional perspective, those from the global north benefited at the expense of those from the global south. Early bioprospecting helped make many European governments and capitalists rich. Not so for European peasants and later industrial workers. However, the movement of crop germplasm from the south to the north did improve the diets of many in the "lower social orders," and as I mentioned, tropical medicines based on southern plant materials protected European soldiers, even if they did not make them rich.

In the global south, recognizing variation by region and, indeed, country, social and economic elites were sometimes able to use colonial structures to legitimize and consolidate their status (Baber 1996). By contrast, indigenous scientific knowledge and related institutions were likely adversely affected by colonial expansion, and the focus on the south as a source for raw material – not manufactured products – provided little, if any, benefit to the "masses" in the global south.

FROM COLONIALISM TO BIOCOLONIALISM

The economic centrality of genetic diversity for the global north and south has an extended and extensive history, as I have described. Today, an array of factors have brought us to a new era in the history of what might be termed bioprospecting or biopiracy (the term one uses, of course, depends on one's political perspective). Dorsey points to four interrelated factors that promoted the current age of bioprospecting: "global, market based economic rationales; rapid and broad technological changes, particularly in biotechnology; a growing interest by pharmaceutical actors to identify their bioprospecting profits with environmental conservation efforts; and efforts to harmonize and standardize global discourses on biodiversity and intellectual property rights regimes" (2001: 271).

Central to the growth of bioprospecting initiatives have been developments in biotechnology. This relatively new technology has created a major impetus to scouring the globe for new sources of genetic material. Among the tools developed have been advanced separation and structure elucidation technology. These technologies routinized the search process and reduced the cost of bioprospecting (Dorsey 2001: 273). With the development of a bioinformatics industry, the DNA of every living creature has become raw material for a huge array of potential products (Kloppenburg 2000: 510). With the promise of intellectual property protection on a world scale assured by global economic bodies, bioprospecting has become even more attractive to industry.

When companies and their representatives from the global north head south, they are aiming to gain access to the vast genetic diversity they know is there, but they are also dependent on the knowledge and labor of peoples who live where this vast genetic diversity is located. Neither the crop plants used by peasant farmers nor the indigenous medicines, which are so attractive to industrial pharmaceutical concerns, are found in nature. On the agricultural front, for thousands of years, while domesticating and maintaining crops, peasant farmers developed a wide range of land races in any one species. A land race is a genetically variable population, where specific types vary in terms of their resistance to pests and disease and their suitability to different environmental conditions. In developing and maintaining land races, peasant farmers engaged in a strategy to produce consistency of production in the face of variation in weather and/or pests. They engaged in informal research year in and year out, comparing the performance of different crop varieties. The result of peasant practices is vast inter- and intra-specific genetic variability within specific and relatively bounded geographic regions. Land races embody farmer knowledge and labor and play a significant role in making industrial agriculture possible. Developments in biotechnology make these land races more accessible than in previous periods to science-based companies from the global north.

In terms of the raw materials for medicines, companies are also dependent on the knowledge and labor of local peoples. As Shultes notes:

> If phytochemists must randomly investigate the constituents of biological effects of 80,000 species of Amazon plants, the task may never be finished. Concentrating first on those species that people have lived and experimented with for millennia offers a short-cut to the discovery of new medically or industrially useful compounds. (Shultes quoted in Moran, King, & Carlson 2001: 512)

Thus, quite commonly, the screening strategies used by corporate bioprospectors draw on knowledge of the traditional use of plants and other materials. Likewise, according to Moran and his colleagues, "leads from the traditional process of plant preparation for healing provide clues to the type of chemical compounds in plants under investigation." Indeed, according to Moran and his collaborators, "of the 120 active compounds isolated from high plants and used today in Western medicine, 74% have the same therapeutic use as in native societies" (Moran, King, & Carlson 2001: 512). More directly, as well, bioprospectors from the north often depend on the knowledge and labor of so-called parataxonomists and para-ecologists – local people who have knowledge from daily experience and traditional understandings passed to them from previous generations – to find and understand genetic resources from the south (Escobar 1997: 49).

One might imagine a highly collaborative relationship between the economic interests of the north and the peasant farmers and traditional medical practitioners from genetically diverse regions of the global south. As I have shown, however, historically this relationship has not been one of equitable collaboration, but instead has been characterized by domination and exploitation. Part of the explanation for the character of this relationship historically has been based on a failure by northern economic interests, and, indeed, national governments, to recognize the value of the knowledge embodied in and associated with the genetic material appropriated from regions of the global south. The conceptual basis of this northern blindness is found in the idea of "common heritage." The idea that colonial plant and other genetic resources were the "common heritage" of humankind was taken for granted by colonial powers and their explorers and researchers. This idea suggests that the genetic material found in plants and other organisms throughout the world is the collective wealth of all human beings and, as a consequence, it may be freely appropriated without payment to the peoples from the regions from which the materials come. The concept treats biological materials found in the global south as "natural." As nature is our human heritage, so these materials are understood to belong, without cost, to all of us. Not recognized as systematic and purposeful innovation, the knowledge and labor of people from the south embodied in this genetic material is not viewed as science or as providing added value to the "natural" biological material. The plants remain, in the view of northern property rights discourse, "natural." Once these materials are altered, however, by certified scientists, they are no longer viewed as common heritage, but as private property.

Common heritage – part of northern property rights discourse – treats only northern scientific knowledge as real, valuable, and ultimately commodifiable, while viewing the knowledge of farmers and traditional medical practitioners effectively not as knowledge at all. This despite the fact that the genetic material appropriated by northern interests would not be valuable to these parties without access to the knowledge associated with it. The notion of common heritage governed the initiatives of northern governments and firms in the appropriation of genetic material from the colonial era until late in the twentieth century. As crises caused by the genetic uniformity of northern agriculture and developments in biotechnology and intellectual property rights prompted increased interest in the genetic resources located in the global south, "the states, bureaucrats, scientists, farmers and indigenous peoples of the South couldn't help but notice that genetic resources that left their hands and lands as free goods were subsequently entering the market and producing income for someone else." The result has been an ongoing struggle over the past two decades in which these groups have sought "to regulate collection or to capture some of the benefit stream from the commercial development of biotic materials" (Kloppenburg 2000: 512).

As the struggle over property rights in genetic material has unfolded in international negotiations and in street protest over the past 20 years or so, questionable cases of appropriation have continued unabated. To take but one example, University of Wisconsin scientists recently patented a protein extracted from the berries of a west African plant known as *Pentadiplandra brazzeana* (Stein 2002: A1). The protein extracted from the berries by Wisconsin scientists is some 2,000 times sweeter than sugar and has almost no calories. Clearly, this is a substance with market potential. Long before the Wisconsin scientists learned of these berries from a French ethnobotanist, their sweet taste had made them a treat for generations of west African peoples. Thus, the discovery of the patented protein was made possible by the traditional knowledge of people whose ancestors had eaten the sugary berries; and, indeed, the ethnobotanist who provided the berries to the Wisconsin scientists acknowledges that his Gabonese assistant first alerted him to the sweetness of the fruit. Officials representing the University of Wisconsin justify not providing compensation by asserting that it is not clear to whom the money should go, especially since the plant from which the berry comes is found in many different countries. In addition, one of the scientists involved said that requiring property negotiations could stifle discovery.

Despite the clear and increasing importance of biological materials from the southern hemisphere over the past 20 years or so, countries and peoples from the global south have been at a systematic and consistent disadvantage in the efforts to reap benefits from the rich genetic diversity of the global south. The contemporary practices and the justifications used by northern governments and multinational companies are shaped by discourses of science and property rights that reflect western notions of legitimate knowledge and capitalist understandings of property. Not meeting the standards traditionally used to designate scientific knowledge, the local and indigenous knowledges which provide the foundation for many of the breakthroughs made by scientists using genetic material from the south are undervalued. These knowledges are quite simply not recognized as knowledge in the same sense that scientific knowledge is knowledge. They are implicitly located lower on a hierarchy of knowledge.

The status of local and indigenous knowledge also affects its recognition as property on the terrain of capitalist economic discourse. In the US, three general criteria make an invention patentable. In the US, these standards, which are broadly the same as those utilized in Europe, are: novelty, non-obviousness, and usefulness. An invention must meet all three criteria to be patentable. While there would be little question that agricultural germplasm or medicinally useful biological materials from the global south meet the last standard – usefulness – there is more question about the other two. Given that these biological materials have typically been used for generations, in the local context they are typically neither novel nor non-obvious. Of course, prior to north–south contact in general or the specific contact and exchange around specific genetic material, the uses of the substances were novel and non-obvious to representatives of the north. In the end, in the western system of intellectual property protection, novelty, and non-obviousness is established through the modern practices of scientists and inventors. Thus, a property rights hierarchy exists in which the capitalist intellectual property regime determines what counts as intellectual property, and what counts is typically produced in the west. Products of local or indigenous knowledge are either not property at all or not property with the same status and protectability as inventions that follow the established intellectual property regime.

TOWARDS EQUITY IN THE EXCHANGE OF BIOLOGICAL RESOURCES

Although the appropriation of biological resources from the south by northern interests continues in some instances without appropriate recognition of, or compensation for, their value, the persistent outrage expressed by representatives of southern countries, communities, and peoples has led to initiatives that aim to improve the equity of north–south relations related to biological resources. In this section, I explore and assess three such initiatives.

Merck, the multinational drug giant, led one of the early initiatives aimed at compensating appropriate groups in the south for the resources and knowledge they provide. In 1991, Merck reached an agreement with the National Institute of Biodiversity (InBio) of Costa Rica, a nonprofit organization (Dorsey 2001: 274). Under the contract, InBio committed to providing Merck with extracts of plants, insects, and micro-organisms from Costa Rica's tropical forests, which could be screened by Merck for chemicals potentially useful in drugs. In exchange, Merck agreed to pay InBio US$1.1 million over 2 years to cover research and sampling expenses. In addition, Merck agreed to provide InBio with royalties resulting from the commercialization of substances derived from Costa Rican biological materials.

Although the Merck agreement embodies a clear recognition of the value of biological materials (and possibly knowledge) located in a country in the southern hemisphere, critics have raised concern because the secret nature of the terms makes it difficult for those concerned about the equity of the arrangement to determine whether it accurately and fairly valuates Costa Rican biological materials. Furthermore, it is not clear why a nonprofit organization rather than the state or ethnic groups from regions from which genetic material is taken should be compensated for provision of genetic resources. Finally, the arrangement is complicated because biodiversity does not recognize national borders, and Merck will not compensate neighboring countries for materials found within their borders as well as in Costa Rica.

While many companies and scientists have taken the position articulated by those associated with the *Pentadiplandra brazzeana* case, arguing that compensation is neither possible nor appropriate, the InBio case indicates there are exceptions. Another exception to this logic is represented by Shaman Pharmaceuticals. The company self-consciously collaborates with local and indigenous peoples in their search for substances of use in new drugs.

Incorporated in 1989, Shaman simultaneously founded a nonprofit organization to develop and implement a process to return benefits to Shaman's 30 collaborating countries and some 60 culture groups, after a product is commercialized. According to one source, "Benefits from commercial products will be shared equally among all countries and culture groups that participate in Shaman's drug discovery process, no matter where the plant or knowledge originated" (Moran, King, & Carlson 2001: 516).

Among the company's commercial successes is Provir, a drug useful in the treatment of AIDS-related diarrhea. As Provir can be used in the treatment of diarrhea with other causes, the company has agreed to donate one bottle of the substance to Direct Relief International for every bottle sold. In addition, Shaman donates an unspecified percentage of its profits from the drug to HIV/AIDS community funding requests (Barnoff 2001).

Still, not all of Shaman's efforts have proceeded smoothly. A federation of Amazon tribes – the Coordinating Committee of Native Organizations of the Amazon Basin – will no longer work with the company after concluding that the firm would not provide sufficient legal protection for indigenous peoples (Lambrecht 1999). Criticisms might also be leveled against Shaman for their failure to make a firm commitment to their southern partners in terms of royalty payments (Posey & Dutfield 1996). Additionally, apparently the company has not considered going as far as considering their local collaborators as co-inventors and sharing patent ownership with them (Posey & Dutfield 1996).

Beyond the initiatives of individual countries and companies, the international Convention on Biodiversity was opened for signature in June of 1992. The Convention – which not surprisingly the United States has refused to sign – is part of the trend toward some sort of recognition of the contributions of the peoples of the global south to the benefits those of us from the north have derived from southern biological materials. The Convention gives nation-states sovereignty over biological resources, thus clearly repudiating the once dominant notion of common heritage. Significantly, it is, like the individual company and country efforts initiated to confront the problem of the equitable distribution and use of genetic resources, based on a deep neoliberal commitment to private property and faith in the superiority of market regulation of resource allocation (Boisvert & Caron 2002: 154). And ultimately, the Convention, while encouraging the equitable sharing of benefits arising from traditional knowledge, does not require it (Moran, King, & Carlson 2001: 519).

These cases notwithstanding, one wonders how much the struggles of the last two decades have really changed things. How much recognition of the value of the biological and knowledge resources from the global south is evident in the efforts of northern nations and firms to quiet the genetic resource wars? Although companies involved in bioprospecting promise to provide a reasonable return to source countries for valuable biologicals, "collectively, pharmaceutical products based on traditional medicine have returned less than 0.0001 per cent of their profits to the local plant users who assisted research and discovery efforts" (Dorsey 2001: 277). What is more, the notions of property on which the entire exchange relationship is premised are fundamentally slanted to the advantage of the north and the disadvantage of the south. Jack Kloppenburg weighs in powerfully on this matter. He argues that "The existing complex of intellectual property rights law is . . . ill-suited to the collective production characteristic of indigenous knowledge" (Kloppenburg 2000: 513). Indeed, intellectual property law is predicated on a romantic notion of the heroic individual inventor (Boyle 1996; Kleinman 2003). It does not contemplate the collective and multi-generational character of knowledge production in many of the regions where genetic diversity is greatest. Kloppenburg suggests, furthermore, that

The farmers and indigenous peoples who are being targeted by the bio-prospectors seldom have experience with the kind of transactions being proposed. Nor do they typically have very extensive knowledge of what bioprospectors will do with the information and organisms they collect, or of the legal, scientific and commercial frameworks into which they are being inserted. Absent such understanding, it is difficult to see how farmers and indigenous peoples can provide informed consent to bioprospecting activities, and it must be difficult for them to construct exchange agreements that are adequately sensitive to their own interests. (2000: 513; see also Boisvert & Caron 2002: 162, 163)

Finally and most broadly, all three of these initiatives are based on bilateral, market-oriented arrangements for compensating peoples of the global south for their knowledge and genetic resources. As Kloppenburg (2004) notes, however, there are many difficulties with such arrangements. I have already pointed to the quandary of providing individual recognition for a collective product, and I have stressed the related difficulties of determining who to compensate in bilateral relations. In addition to these problems, it is difficult to establish a price for genetic materials. The value of a particular specimen cannot be determined when it is collected. Evaluation, research, and development are required before a commercial concern will know its value, and in fact, some traits may not be of recognized value until well after the collection of the material. In short, while all three arrangements mark a step forward in that they recognize genetic resources and the knowledge yoked to them as valuable, they all suffer from shortcomings and do not establish an equitable playing field.

CONCLUSIONS

In this chapter, I outlined the history of colonial relations around biological resources. I showed that the biological resources from the southern hemisphere were crucial to the development of the economies of the colonial powers of the north and were part and parcel of a process of asymmetrical political, economic, and scientific relations between these two regions of the world. I suggested that the colonial appropriation of genetic resources from the global south was part of a wider process which undermined the economic development of the south. In addition, I considered how current trends in bioprospecting (or biopiracy) reflect the history of colonial domination of the global south by countries of the north and are shaped by notions of property, knowledge, and invention that advantage actors from the global north over peoples of the south.[1] Finally, I briefly explained three recent efforts to compensate peoples of the south for their genetic resources and knowledge, and outlined some of their shortcomings.

I have suggested that early colonial history was part of broader trends that established definitions of capitalist property and scientific knowledge. The dominant discourses of property and knowledge have led to the systematic undervaluing of the knowledge and related biological resources from the global south by economic interests from the north. Like so many developments in the technoscientific realm, the matter of biological resources raises fundamental questions about equity. It is, of course, an oversimplification to suggest that the north benefits and the south loses in these relations. Some in the south allied with northern economic interests benefit from the current structure of relations and the dominant discourses of science-based property, and average citizens from northern countries do not derive benefits at the same level as, for example, pharmaceutical industry executives do. Still, I would suggest this is fundamentally a north–south issue. Its resolution will demand that adherents to dominant ideas about what counts as scientific knowledge take another look. We must recognize that knowledge production is a broadly collective endeavor in which different individuals and groups contribute but "partial perspectives" (Haraway 1988) to what is fundamentally a knowledge commons. Without any given partial perspective, knowledge production cannot proceed in the same manner. Once we recognize the value of different varieties of knowledge, we need to reconsider how they should be compensated for. As I argue in chapter 4, it is not clear that the intellectual property protection promotes innovation. Thus, if we want to promote innovation in the interest of the world population, compensation for all parties based on the established system of intellectual property protection may not be the appropriate way to proceed.

NOTES

1   While I focus on the ownership and equity issues related to bioprospecting, questions have been raised about ecological sustainability associated with these relations. See Lacy (2003).

6

Gender and the Ideology of Merit: Women, Men, Science, and Engineering

I have contended throughout this book that technoscience is social. In chapter 1, I suggested that there are many ways in which we might think of the meaning of "social." In this chapter, the most important way to think about technoscience as social is in terms of the norms and social common sense that orient our behavior. These are shaped by social forces typically beyond our control as individual human beings. They are taken on across lifetimes of people, often with little consciousness or reflection, and they constrain the way in which people act and the opportunities open to them. In this chapter, it is our social common sense about merit and gender that concern me. In addition to the importance of normative and cognitive orientation to the world being social, in this chapter we see as well that organizational structures – again external to individuals and constraining upon them – play an important role in shaping the opportunities and limits women and men face in science.

My central focus in this chapter is the divergent experiences of men and women in science and engineering training and careers. I begin the chapter by criticizing the idea that the world of science is meritocratic. The idea that many, if not most, institutions in the US operate according to criteria of merit is a variety of social common sense. We accept it unthinkingly. I challenge the idea that science is a meritocracy and show instead the array of social and gendered factors that affect the career experiences of women and men in technoscience. I consider these experiences in academia and science-based industry. I conclude the chapter by showing that gender – simultaneously a social structure and a form of common sense – shapes not only the career trajectories of men and women in science and engineering but also the character of technological artifacts and the substance of science.

"MERIT" AND STRATIFICATION IN SCIENCE

The view that the US is, broadly speaking, a land of equal opportunity, where one's fortune is determined by hard work and individual merit, is widely held. This is a notion that stresses the capacity of individuals and ignores the structural factors that affect one's life chances. Among social scientists there is a broad, if uneven, consensus, that the notion that "anyone can make it" in this nation is fundamentally a myth (see, for example, MacLeod 1995; Featherman & Hauser 1978). This is not to say that poor children never grow up to be affluent professionals or for that matter that children from affluent backgrounds never end up as poor, under-educated adults. However, the chances of educational, occupational, and economic success are much higher for the children of the educated and the wealthy than for the children of the poor and less educated. Better schools and extracurricular educational opportunities, the social networks to which the better-off belong, the availability of second chances, and a myriad of other factors all increase the prospects of the children of the well-off in comparison to the children of the poor. At the same time, the barriers to success faced by children from lower-income backgrounds are also sub-stantial. Poor schools, few extracurricular opportunities, leveled aspira-tions, and systematic bias are just a few of the impediments to success that children from lower-income backgrounds face (MacLeod 1995; Kozol 1991).

If the American social and economic system is not strictly speaking gov-erned by merit and achievement, it has been widely claimed that the insti-tution of science embodies all we strive for in the broader society: it is a meritocracy. Probably the most prominent statement of this position is artic-ulated by Robert K. Merton. For Merton, three norms guarantee that the most qualified will succeed in science. First, science is governed by univer-salism. The idea here is that all claims to truth are subjected to *"preestab-lished impersonal criteria"* (1973: 270). According to this line of reasoning, the best scientific research will be recognized as such no matter the back-ground of the researcher. Evaluation processes, according to this norm, are impersonal. It is the work that matters, not the individual.

A second attribute of science, according to Merton, is disinterestedness. Centrally, because the results of science are verifiable by the community of scientists, evaluation of research is likely to be unbiased. By extension, the work of each scientist should be assessed on its merits. Evaluation of the quality of a scientist's work should not be biased by her personal characteristics.

Finally, Merton argued that science is governed by "organized skepti-cism." This is the idea that science is shaped by "the temporary suspension of judgment and the detached scrutiny of beliefs" (1973: 277). In other words, one's achievement will not be prejudged based on factors beyond the work itself. Again, this norm should lead science to operate according to a logic of merit.[1]

Early work by followers of Merton attempted to empirically illustrate that science is, indeed, a meritocracy. In their 1973 book, *Stratification in Science*, Jonathan and Steven Cole assumed that science is "both rationally and universalistically organized" and that, as a consequence "the criteria for judgment will be the quality of a scientist's research and his performance in roles which directly contribute to furthering scientific goals" (1973: 66). Thus, drawing on the data from the *Science Citation Index*, the authors contend that two-thirds of the variance on awards received by scientists (that is, the difference in the number and kind of rewards received by individual scientists) is explained by differences in research quality (1973: 93). They found, furthermore, that "those men who have produced the best research and who work at the best departments" will be the most visible scientists (1973: 102). For the physicist, according to the Coles, the quality of "scientific work, as evaluated by his colleagues, is the single most important determinant of whether he rises to a position of eminence or remains obscure" (1973: 122).

In the matter of the differences in the experiences of men and women in science, the authors come to several conclusions. First, while there is "some measure of sex-related particularism" in the reward system of science – that is, that sex affects the rewards one receives to some degree – there is "little discrimination against women scientists after receipt of the Ph.D." (1973: 146). Second, there is little evidence that women suffer from cumulative disadvantage (1973: 149). In other words, lacking the resources that provide a foundation for success in science at an earlier point in time does not have a cumulatively adverse effect on success later. Finally, according to the authors, it is the larger society – and its nonmeritocratic norms – that ultimately explain the differences in male and female success in science, not the character of the scientific field itself.

For many years, this kind of research had a high profile in the analysis of stratification in science. I would suggest, however, that its underlying logic is fundamentally flawed. Willing to acknowledge the social character of science at the margins, but not at the heart of the enterprise, the Coles and others assume what they must show – that science is a meritocracy. And any divergence from the meritocratic character of science is justified as in the interest of the effective and efficient functioning of the institution.

At a very basic level, the measure of the primary causal factor the Coles use to explain the differential success of scientists is problematic. The authors's essential conclusion is that, although there are some intervening factors, the most important predictor of success in science is the *quality* of one's work. The problem is with the measure of quality. If there were an intrinsic measure of quality and it were possible to measure it, then we could ascertain whether the most qualified persons in a given field were the most successful. The difficulty is that no such measure exists. Instead, the Coles measure quality in terms of the number of citations a scientist's published research receives. While it is true that citation counts can measure the recognition a scientist receives and the impact her work has, there is no reason to assume that the "best" work is the most cited. Indeed, one could imagine that the most cutting-edge work would be systematically ignored because of the threat it posed to the careers of those in the status quo (Kuhn 1962).

What counts as best – what is viewed as high-quality research – is fundamentally a social matter. In fields with high levels of contention, there will be disagreement about what counts as quality, but even where there is no disagreement, it is members of a field and not something about the work itself that defines research quality. If this is the case and women's work is rated as lower quality than men's, the explanation for this rating may not be about the work itself but about the people doing the work. This problem is equally true for the question of "originality," another supposed determinant of success in science. People determine what counts as original, not something about the work itself. Indeed, what counts as original in one era may not be viewed as such in another (Sperber 1990). And again, just as scientists may disagree about what counts as a competent experiment (Collins & Pinch 1993), they may equally disagree about what counts as original work. Even where they do not, it is the people not the work that determine quality.

As I suggested in the first chapter of this book, following Pierre Bourdieu, science is a field like any other. It is a field in which power and opportunity, and thus stratification, are socially structured. In the pages that follow, I traverse recent research on the relationship between gender and scientific training and work – both in academia and industry – and show the ways in which social structure fundamentally shapes the experiences of men and women in science.

WOMEN, MEN, AND ACADEMIC SCIENCE

The scholarly literature on gender and science is vast, and I do not intend to review it here. Instead, I will draw on a selection of it to highlight what are widely believed to be the most important factors in explaining the divergent experiences of men and women in academic science and engineering training and careers. What I will suggest is that science is a fundamentally social institution. Although I distinguish between factors external and internal to the scientific field in explaining the divergent experiences of men and women, this distinction is ultimately artificial, and it makes little sense to argue that while the larger social world is not meritocratic, the internal world of science is. Instead, I suggest that the two "worlds" are inseparable. Practices and values from outside shape what happens inside. Thus, for example, gender socialization begins outside of science, but shapes how men and women act in science. But, in addition, even the practices within science itself show it to be a fundamentally social field.

There are more women today in academic science and engineering than there were just a few decades ago, but men and women have by no means achieved parity. In 1995, some 38 percent of students in science and engineering graduate school were women (Etzkowitz, Kemelgor, & Uzzi 2000: 11). Significantly, there is important variation by discipline, with women representing only 19 percent of graduate students in mathematics, 12 percent in physics, and 11 percent in engineering (ibid.: 11). According to Xie and Shauman (2003: 152), by 1990 approximately a third of practicing scientists in math and biology were women, while about 25 percent of physicists were women and 10 percent of engineers were women. Significantly, women's representation in science and technology careers declines as they proceed up the career ladder (Etzkowitz, Kemelgor, & Uzzi 2000: 13).

If the scientific field were a meritocracy, the different experiences of men and women would be explicable in terms of their different capacities. However, there is not good evidence of clear-cut differences in the behavior of newborns (Etzkowitz, Kemelgor, & Uzzi 2000: 37), and existing evidence suggests that "innate differences in scientific ability between men and women are nonexistent or very small" (Xie & Shauman 2003: 5). In fact, "although women's attainments in science are lower than men's, their [women Ph.D.'s's] measured ability (IQ) is actually higher" (Fox 1995: 217). In addition, recent work by Xie and Shauman indicates that "gender differences in expected [postsecondary] participation in [science and engineering] education cannot be attributed to gender differences in academic achievement" (2003: 70).

If innate differences between men and women and achievement differences are not the primary explanations for the divergent experiences of women and men in science and engineering, something else must be going on. My consideration of possible factors will follow the human life-course, beginning by looking at gender socialization and then turning to the experience of women and men in education, and finally to careers in science and engineering.

Social scientists commonly make a distinction between gender and sex. They argue that gender should be thought of as a social product, whereas it might be possible to think about sex as biological or anatomical category

(Lorber 1994). Socialization into gender roles, then, is often understood to begin at birth. To take but one study, Pomerleau and his colleagues found powerful evidence of the emergence of gender differences in infancy. Using data on a sample of 78 healthy infants and their parents, the authors investigated the physical environment (toys, clothing, accessories, and room decor) of boys and girls at three ages during the first years of life. Even at this young age, the researchers found that more girls than boys (85 percent vs. 68 percent) had dolls, while more boys than girls (37 percent vs. 17 percent) had tools. At 25 months, more girls than boys possessed kitchen appliances and utensils (55 percent vs. 15 percent). More generally, girls owned more toys categorized as feminine (80 percent vs. 60 percent) and boys had more masculine toys (40 percent vs. 12 percent). Finally, according to the participating parents, boys wore more blue, red, and white than girls, who wore more pink and multicolored clothes. We do not know the impact of these differences in treatment between very young girls and boys later in their lives; however, it seems perfectly reasonable to speculate, as Pomerleau and his colleagues do, that "Infants who are encouraged and reinforced to play with dolls and child's furniture, or sports equipment and tools, will be more likely to choose these objects when they have a choice" (1990: 366). More importantly, these kinds of experiences may shape the kinds of choices young men and women make later in life by defining what they view as appropriate for people of their gender.

Analysts of the experience of men and women in science stress the importance of gender socialization in shaping the divergent experiences of these two groups (Xie & Shauman 2003: 17; Etzkowitz, Kemelgor, & Uzzi 2000: 32ff.). In a small study of 53 children aged 2 to 6, Etzkowitz and his colleagues found that boys were more likely than girls to see themselves as scientists, and boys tended to have more negative attitudes about the idea of women as scientists than girls. Suggesting the cumulative effects of gender socialization, the older boys studied were less likely than younger boys to see girls as possible future scientists (Etzkowitz, Kemelgor, & Uzzi 2000: 34). More generally, "children above the age of three could identify scientific and medical occupational roles and had begun to link occupations with sex based on their knowledge of their family and the outside world" (Etzkowitz, Kemelgor, & Uzzi 2000: 35).

Early school experiences too can shape the choices boys and girls make about science, their capacity to make independent choices on such matters, and even their preparation to face postsecondary scientific training. Some research has suggested that teachers treat boys and girls differently in classroom settings, accepting aggressive or assertive behavior in boys, but not in girls (Sadker and Sadker 1994). Earlier work found that teachers encouraged exploration, autonomy and development of independent math skills in boys, but discouraged them in girls (Birns 1976). Still other research provides evidence that boys are encouraged to engage in tinkering behavior, while girls are not (McIlwee & Robinson 1992). In sum, while men and women may enter postsecondary education with similar formal preparation and even qualification, their gender socialization will mean that at an informal level their preparation is likely to be different. They may hold different ideas about their abilities and have developed different skills in preparing to navigate the postsecondary school environment.

If socialization and early school experience were the only factors that affected the divergent science career trajectories of men and women, it might be possible to contend that factors in the larger nonmeritocratic world may disadvantage women, but a universalistic system based on criteria of merit shapes the careers of men and women once they reach the university. However, in the university itself, a set of social processes differentially affect male and female students.

Once in university, young men and women interested in science and engineering face a system of courses designed to weed out all but the "strongest" students (Etzkowitz, Kemelgor, & Uzzi 2000: 49ff.; Hacker 1990: 149). Strength here does not necessarily mean capacity to do the work in math and science. Instead, the system is premised on values traditionally coded as male, most centrally competition and ongoing challenge. In other words, it is an environment in which competitive behavior – as against, for example, cooperative behavior – is highly valued and shapes processes. The type of support from teachers found in high school education is lacking, and, according to Etzkowitz and his colleagues, "women whose education was grounded in a different system of values, produce feelings of rejection, discouragement, and lowered self-confidence" in this new environment (Etzkowitz, Kemelgor, & Uzzi 2000: 49). Because of their respective backgrounds, women may find it more difficult than men to succeed in this environment.

In graduate school, the weeding process continues with a system some women find harsher and more discouraging than what they experienced in college (Etzkowitz, Kemelgor, & Uzzi 2000: 50). At both undergraduate and graduate levels, any weeding process works through the interaction of an ostensibly objective process of selecting the most talented students and the prior socialization experience of the students who face the weeding. Again, if this factor alone were responsible for the divergent educational and professional experiences of men and women, one might be able to conclude that while the world outside science is rife with inequitable processes, within science there is a meritocracy. However, at the graduate level, two other factors become crucial. The first is integration of students into informal networks, and the second is regular support from faculty mentors. The centrality of informal networks to graduate schools's success contradicts the idea that the scientific field is a meritocracy that operates according to impersonal and universalistic criteria. A wide-ranging literature points to the importance of networks for success in science education, and there is little question that everything from the ability to participate in such networks to the resources that they provide participants are informal and implicit. Etzkowitz et al. succinctly and cogently describe the nature and operation of informal networks:

> An unofficial doctoral education process, based on the establishment of informal ties, runs parallel to the official degree program of formal instruction, examinations, and research production. Informal support structures and social gatherings provide information, encouragement and, most importantly, opportunities to learn from peers and role models in unpressured settings. (2000: 73)

Students gain support, which is important, but they also gain access to information, which they might not otherwise obtain. Etzkowitz and his colleagues go on to point out that students in networks learn departmental lore and about the idiosyncrasies of faculty members – information that might find its way into examinations and may affect student treatment in laboratories and classrooms (2000: 73).

Such networks are often less open to women, and while student-based networks may make it easier for students to make it through graduate school, networks that extend beyond students can also affect students once they receive their Ph.D.s. Exclusion from impromptu dinners and drinking evenings, from sporting events and the like, may leave women without the professional contacts that are absolutely crucial to finding postdoctoral fellowships and academic employment. According to Etzkowitz et al., "Few women who attain advanced degrees acquire the density of connections that typically accrue to men as they move into the academic system" (2000: 100). Outside these networks, women are less likely to have connections to scholarly journal editors, officers of professional associations, and reviewers of grants. They are less likely to appear on programs of national meetings or to be invited to lecture or consult outside their own university (Fox 1995: 220). Women scientists may also have more difficulty than men in finding collaborators and establishing collaborative relationships (Fox 1995: 221). These kinds of connections are important for career advancement. Beyond affecting feelings of inclusion and isolation, they may have a very concrete "bearing on productivity and on the productivity differences between men and women" (Fox 1995: 220). In sum, here is a mechanism that while drawing on attitudes that surely begin outside of the scientific field is at its core nonuniversalistic. It is premised on implicit and informal attitudes and works at the heart of science to shape career experience.

Mentors are also crucial to academic success in science and engineering. Fox argues that given the highly decentralized character of graduate education in the sciences, the advisor–advisee relationship is the "core of graduate education" (2000: 57). Recognition and encouragement of talent is important to self-esteem and ultimately academic and professional success. Here again, while departments may formally assign advisers to graduate students, rapport between student and faculty member determines the quality of and the benefits from a mentoring relationship. A good adviser encourages her or his students, provides direction, and helps develop successful strategies for navigating graduate school and the transition to professional life. Well-networked mentors can provide their students with access to information that is not publicly available about, for example, jobs and cutting-edge research underway, and invitations to present work at prestigious conferences (Etzkowitz et al. 2000: 123).

In their work, Etzkowitz and his colleagues found that "many male advisors offer support to male students, but leave women to figure out things for themselves" (2000: 86). Their female respondents reported feeling lost and incompetent without the support of a faculty mentor (2000: 100). Other research has found that women graduate students are less likely than their male counterparts to see faculty members and advisers frequently. Women report that their relationships with faculty are less relaxed and egalitarian than do men. In addition, men are more likely than women to say they are viewed seriously by professors, and men are more likely than women to say they regard themselves as colleagues of faculty, instead of students (Fox 1995: 218, reports relevant studies). At a general level, Etzkowitz and his colleagues contend that those who had positive relationships with advisers were more likely to thrive in graduate students than those who do not (2000: 147).

Once in academic jobs, the experiences of men and women differ in several ways. Two seem especially important: participation in networks and families. Ph.D. in hand and out among professional scientists and engineers, academics depend on networks for the exchange of ideas, information, and resources that are not formally circulated in journals, requests for research proposals and the like (Etzkowitz et al. 2000: 121). Murmann and Landau's work suggests that network linkages stimulate innovation and quality research (1998). Through informal networks one can learn about jobs not yet formally announced and research areas that might be of high priority interest to a funder. One can also learn what colleagues think about the quality of research undertaken by others in a given field, and one can make connections with possible collaborators, or with scientists interested in similar research areas or with different but related skills (Seashore, Blumenthal, Gluck, & Soto 1989). Etzkowitz and his colleagues conclude that "Network structures composed of an intermediate level of strong department ties and a large network of bridging ties beyond the department are consistently associated with publishing [of research findings] by improving the ability of a researcher both to gain access to novel information that is circulating in other networks and to collaborate productively with close ties within the department on research projects," and that lacking placement in the proper structure of network relations is an important barrier to the success of women in science (2000: 176). This conclusion is confirmed by other researchers as well (see Fox 2001: 660).

The nature of networks and mentoring in science and engineering suggests that the scientific field operates through something akin to the "homosocial" process described by Kanter (1977) at work in corporate settings. Like in the corporate world, many of the decisions made in the scientific community cannot be based on formal, explicit rules. Instead, male scientists – mentors and colleagues – must draw on informal judgments of the likely behavior of women students and colleagues. These judgments are likely to be based on their prior assumptions about gender and gendered behavior. More generally, men are simply likely to be more comfortable working with people who are like them: other men. The result is that mentors and colleagues may serve to reproduce the system of science in ways that are familiar from their experience before they entered science and the experience of the system of science established by their male predecessors. Men inadvertently may help reproduce a nonmeritocratic system that works to the advantage of other men.

Research findings on the effect of marriage and family on the relative success of men and women in science and engineering education and careers are among the clearest and most unambiguous of all research done on gender and science and engineering. Drawing on a broad array of representative data, Xie and Shauman found "a clear and persistent pattern in which marriage and parenthood exacerbate gender differences, even after controlling for a variety of demographic and human capital explanatory factors. Gender differences among unmarried scientists are either small or nonexistent, but married women experience large disadvantages relative to men, especially if they have children" (2003: 152). The authors argue that "the careers of men benefit from marriage and parenthood, while the careers of women are impeded by family responsibilities" (152). Xie and Shauman found that family responsibilities make it less likely that women will participate in graduate education or pursue careers in science and engineering education (117). Once in careers, the gap between the amount of time devoted to work decreases among married female scientists relative to men in science and engineering. According to Xie and Shauman's research, "women with very young children work about 25 percent fewer hours than their male counterparts" (171). Beyond this, family life restricts the mobility of female sciences much more than it does for men. Married men, in other words, are freer to pursue the best jobs, wherever they are available, than are married women, and Xie and Shauman conclude that women's more limited mobility is probably due to their primary role in caregiving (175).

Xie and Shauman's findings on marriage, family, and science and technology are echoed in the work of Etzkowitz and his colleagues (2000: 87–91, 134–43) and reflect what Arlie Hochchild (1990) has dubbed the "second shift." According to Hochchild, working women in the US in family settings do 60 to 80 percent of all housework. Put differently, the average woman with a full-time job in a two-career couple works an extra month of 24-hour days each year. This is the "second shift," and it occurs at a time when women are increasingly moving into the workforce and holding down full-time jobs. A "stalled revolution" has occurred in which it is widely considered acceptable for women to work outside the home, but there has not been a similar shift in attitude about household labor, childcare, and the relationship between the workplace and the home (Hochschild 1989).

Our attitudes about gender roles are changing, but changing unevenly and slowly, and in the highly competitive world of academic science and engineering this puts women at a significant disadvantage compared to men. As Xie and Shauman show, being married with children hurts women and helps men. Women have less time to work, men more. Etzkowitz and colleagues suggest that beyond the attitudes in society at large that affect the work time available to men and women in science and engineering and affect their relative mobility, there are attitudes within the scientific field, surely drawn from outside, that also adversely affect women. Etzkowitz et al. found that "Women, but not men, are sometimes thought to be less than serious about their science if they do not stay single while in graduate school" (2000: 88). In addition, they found that in most academic science departments they studied, there is a strong bias against women combining parenthood and an academic career (2000: 91). Finally, Etzkowitz et al. suggest that while a gap in one's academic career as a result of child-birth or child-rearing is not supposed to be officially taken into account in hiring and promotion decisions, it is often "taken into account to a woman's detriment" (2000: 135).

In the end, in understanding the quite divergent experiences of men and women in science and engineering, it is impossible to say that the scientific field operates as a meritocracy, because it does not exist in isolation from the larger social world. While it is true that people enter science with attitudes that develop well prior to their entry, and that these may affect their experiences in science, it is also the case that the mechanisms that shape careers within science are based on informal rules and conventions that are guided by deep-seated gendered perspectives. Thus, while creating a more equitable experience for women in science and engineering will surely be facilitated by the establishment of formal mechanisms and procedures that self-consciously seek to root out gender bias, until broader social attitudes change, the scientific field will not even approximate a meritocracy.

In concluding this section, I need to offer two important cautions. First, while there is a great deal of research on gender and science, like most scholarship, this work has limitations. The samples from which conclusions are drawn are often limited – based on a relatively small region, limited number of universities or university types, or covering a limited time period. Thus, we must treat any conclusion with caution. In addition, although I have treated science and engineering as a homogeneous field, there is substantial variation. Women fare better in some disciplines than in others.

WOMEN AND MEN IN SCIENCE-BASED INDUSTRY

While the scholarly literature on male and female scientists with university careers is, as I have said, vast, the research on men and women in science-based industry is, by comparison, quite limited. In this section I draw on two studies on the topic that come to apparently contradictory conclusions about the factors that affect the career mobility of women in science-based industry. One explores the experience of women and men in engineering-based firms in the 1980s, and the other looks at the experience of female and male scientists in the biotechnology industry in the 1990s.

I begin with a discussion of the research of Judith McIlwee and J. Gregg Robinson (McIlwee & Robinson 1992; Robinson & McIlwee 1989). These scholars studied the job status and career mobility patterns of female and male engineers in mechanical and electrical engineering, aerospace, and high-technology industries. A major source of their data was responses to a questionnaire mailed to a random sample of electrical and mechanical engineering graduates from two public universities in southern California. Because all of their respondents received their engineering degrees at the same time, any difference in job status or career mobility between men and women cannot be explained by differences in years since graduation. Similarly, because, formally at least, these engineers received the same education, this cannot be used to explain differences in career experiences.

Still, despite similar educational backgrounds, only a few years out of school and in their first postgraduation jobs, differences in job statuses between male and female subjects in McIlwee and Robinson's study had already emerged. 58 percent of men worked in the high status area of design, while only 43 percent of women did. Some 20 percent of men were in supervisory positions, while only 15 percent of women were. Finally, Robinson and McIlwee found that women were less likely than men to move up the status and supervisory hierarchies and more likely to move down (Robinson & McIlwee 1989: 457).

Beyond these broad findings are an interesting set of differences in the experiences of the men and women McIlwee and Robinson studied. The authors found that the occupational experiences of men and women varied by industry and engineering specialty, with women doing better in aerospace and mechanical engineering and less well in high-tech and electrical engineering.

The industry finding is particularly perplexing because the general culture in aerospace is often regarded as particularly sexist, and one might imagine that in a new industry (high-tech) with a younger population of workers the culture would be more generally forward-thinking. Why then, McIlwee and Robinson ask, "do we find women in higher status jobs in the more sexist atmosphere of the aerospace firm" (Robinson & McIlwee 1989: 460)? An important part of the answer, according to the researchers, is to be found in the different organizational structures of the two kinds of firms. Aerospace firms are large and tend to be bureaucratic. Job descriptions, avenues of authority and communication, and measures for mobility are formally specified. That is, the rules for behavior at work and job promotion are explicit and clear. In addition, these firms rely on government contracts and consequently must follow affirmative-action regulations. By contrast, high-tech firms are more likely to be smaller and so less bureaucratic, with fewer formal rules, and are less likely to have government contracts.

According to Robinson and McIlwee, a formal bureaucratic structure appears to facilitate "mobility for women. Its formalism means that the 'rules of the game' are clear. The newcomer in a non-traditional field can quickly learn the rules, and can rely on formal structures and qualifications as she seeks to advance" (1989: 461). Adherence to formal rules and procedures appears to protect women from the apparently sexist culture in precisely the way in which formal bureaucracies are supposed to protect those who work in them and are affected by them from arbitrary treatment (Weber 1978). By contrast, the less formal structures in high-tech industry appear to hurt female engineers. Robinson and McIlwee describe the organizational character of these firms as "ambiguous and informal." They suggest that

> The rapid growth of the industry and the importance of innovation within it means that change is constant, job assignments are vague and open-ended, authority relations frequently shift and overlap, and formal channels of communication are rare. The non-routine work in these organizations places an emphasis on autonomy and initiative, and means that personal reputations and peer evaluations count more for advancement than formal requirements. (1989: 461)

Recent work by Laurel Smith-Doerr (2004) is in some ways similar to McIlwee and Robinson's research. Like McIlwee and Robinson, Smith-Doerr looks at the ways in which organizational setting appears to affect the work experience of women, although in her case the focus is on life-scientists, not engineers, and Smith-Doerr's findings are quite different than McIlwee and Robinson's.

Smith-Doerr analyzes the careers of more than 2,000 life-scientists in the United States and supplements her analysis of this data with interviews of 41 scientists. She is interested in professional mobility – career promotion – and compares the experiences of women in what she terms network and hierarchical organizations. She describes the former as having flatter hierarchies and more permeable and fluid boundaries than the latter. These are the organizations that McIlwee and Robinson see as having fewer formal rules and less clear authority relationships; the ones in which women are likely to have fewer successes in McIlwee and Robinson's data. Smith-Doerr notes that such organizations are typically relatively small and often rely on cross-departmental teams; their structures are closely tied to the need for rapid and high levels of innovation.

In general, like McIlwee and Robinson, Smith-Doerr found that men experience greater mobility than women in life-science careers. In Smith Doerr's study, "Being female is associated with a 32 percent decrease in one's odds of attaining a leadership position" (2004: 16). This is true holding constant or controlling for differences in years since these scientists received their Ph.D.s and the status of the universities where they received their degrees.

While, overall, women do less well than men in both networked and hierarchical firms, women's likelihood of achieving a supervisory position is much lower in what Smith-Doerr calls nonbiotech (typically hierarchical) organizations than in biotech (typically networked) organizations. According to Smith-Doerr, "Female PhDs in biotech firms are nearly 8 *times* as likely to be in leadership positions than female PhDs in more hierarchical organizations" (2004: 17). Smith-Doerr's quantitative data does not explain this finding, but drawing on her interviews she tentatively concludes that network structures appear to offer more open opportunities for women. Less hierarchical structures, according to Smith-Doerr, appear to provide "more varied opportunity for all scientists to take positions of responsibility" (2004: 21) and to do challenging work. In addition, Smith-Doerr argues that the transparency of network organizations (the ability of those in these organizations to see how they operate), resulting form its relatively flat structure and the network of relations within and beyond the firm, produces the same kinds of accountability that might exist in highly formal bureaucracies. Finally, team organization improves women's likelihood of success by making rewards more collective and less individualized (2004: 26).

How do we square these results, and what lessons might we draw from them? First, one might conclude that organizational structure by itself is not what created opportunity for the female life-scientists in Smith-Doerr's study. Highly flexible structures might create opportunities for women, but they do not inevitably do so, as we can see by comparing Smith-Doerr's life-scientists with McIlwee and Robinson's engineers in high-tech industry. It may be that the *culture* in engineering-related flat organizations is more sexist than what we might find in life-science firms. As a result, women are adversely affected by informal structures in engineering and have opportunities in informal structures in the biological sciences. In addition, the nature of supervision may differ in the engineering and life-science fields and even within fields. One could imagine that in flat life-science firms there are a disproportionately large number of supervisory positions, whereas this could be less true in engineering-related high-tech and in drug firms. Finally, we must read Smith-Doerr's results cautiously, as they may be muddied by the fact that she lumps all biotechnology firms together, and her category of bureaucratic organizations puts large drug companies in the same group as universities. There is likely a great deal of difference between firms within the biotechnology industry (cf. Kleinman & Vallas forthcoming), and similarly, the organizational and career mobility structures in pharmaceutical firms and universities are very likely quite different. Smith-Doerr's data does not really tell us anything about the structures of the firms and universities from which she has data. We can only speculate based on what other research has shown about the structure of these organizations. Overall, I suspect that informal structures *can* work to the advantage of female scientists when the culture is not sexist; however, formal rules central to bureaucratic structures are more likely to protect women from informal sexism than the supposed transparency of network organizations.

BEYOND STRATIFICATION IN SCIENCE AND ENGINEERING: ARTIFACTS AND RESEARCH AS GENDERED

My focus in this chapter has been on the politics of gender in the training and career experiences of scientists and engineers. However, this politics plays itself out in an array other technoscientific-related arenas. In the next several paragraphs, I would like to touch on a few.

To begin with, the character of technology has been shaped in myriad ways by what we might term social structures of gender. An early example of this is the development of bicycle technology in Victorian England.

Gender norms specific to a particular period are diffused throughout societies. They constitute the social common sense and are taken for granted by many members of a given society (Lorber 1994). Thus, in the case of the bicycle, Woodforde (1970) describes the social context within which both manufacturers and riders found themselves: "the whole weight of late Victorian propriety set itself against the adoption by women of . . . [a] masculine and revealing posture" (1970: 144). Thus, manufacturers developed bicycles that would not upset notions of appropriate behavior by women and would not reveal parts of their bodies that Victorians expected to remain covered. The physical character of Victorian bicycles was shaped by notions of gender taken for granted at the time.

The case of military aircraft cockpit design similarly reflects unexamined assumptions about gender. Here, however, the question is not about propriety but about who is capable of flying military aircraft. According to Rachel Weber,

> Civilian and defense aircraft have traditionally been built to male specifications . . . Since women tend to be shorter, have smaller limbs and less upper-body strength, some may not be accommodated by such systems and may experience difficulty reaching controls and operating certain types of equipment. (1999)

US military design criteria for aircraft led to the development of cockpits that will accommodate 90 percent of men, but not be useable by many women. No doubt this reflects a set of unexamined assumptions by the developers of these criteria about who pilots are and what makes a good pilot. Criteria developers certainly assume – probably on the basis of male domination of military aircraft flight – that men will be the users of these aircraft. Here not only do gender assumptions shape the design of aircraft, but equally they are likely to have the effect of limiting the opportunities women might have for careers in aviation in the Navy or Air Force even as those norms change (Weber 1999: 375).

In addition to how gender structures artifacts, it also has had profound effects on the substance of science. Thus, for example, in her research Emily Martin (1991) has shown the ways in which unwarranted gendered assumptions shaped how biologists thought about reproduction from early in the twentieth century. Socially held assumptions about gender historically led to the characterization of men as active and women as passive. These assumptions have often been extended beyond men and women to other living beings and biological processes. Thus, scientists viewed sperm as active and eggs as passive. There is good evidence that both sperm and egg play active roles in the fertilization process; however, this imagery continues to shape thinking about the reproduction process, and this gendering of sperm and eggs limits the capacity of biologists to understand the role of each in fertilization.

According to Bonnie Spanier (e.g. 1995), social stereotypes of men and women are often extended to biological phenomena by scientists. Thus, the nucleus of the cell is often characterized as male and the cytoplasm as female. Classical genetics focuses on nuclear heredity, understood as male, and neglects cytoplasmic heredity, seen as female. And scientists designate the development or nondevelopment of testis (male) as the marker of biological sex in humans and animals, instead of using the development of female genitalia as the "sex determination" marker. Spanier argues further that viewing DNA as the master molecule of life, a formulation that emerged in the 1950s, is at once a fundamentally male designation, since it implies hierarchy and centralization (organizational characteristics often associated with men) and has led to a fundamentally reductionistic biology that fails to consider the complex system of interactions in which living things exist.

In the last several paragraphs, I have attempted to move beyond the focus of this chapter to suggest that technoscience is fundamentally gendered. I have suggested that the physical shape and operation of technological artifacts can be affected by taken-for-granted gendered norms of propriety and the division of labor (who does what job). Following the work of scholars like Martin and Spanier, I have suggested that gendered metaphors can affect how scientists think about research problems. In the case of the artifacts discussed, we can see that our gendered social common sense can shape divergent opportunities for men and women through the technologies they can use and how they use them. Finally, in scientific research, gendered metaphors which imply assumptions about male/female relations can lead to partial, incomplete, and sometimes incorrect understandings (Harding 1986).

CONCLUSIONS

Drawing on an extensive literature, I spent the bulk of this chapter showing the multiple ways in which gender infuses the training and career structures of science and engineering. Although those who participate in the technoscientific enterprise might wish for a world characterized by the Mertonian norms of universalism and disinterestedness, on the gender front this is simply not the world we live in. One might argue that, insofar as the divergent experiences of men and women in science and engineering are affected by their gender socialization prior to entering the scientific field, merit and achievement might still govern the allocation of persons. However, I have shown that the line between what happens outside of science and what happens within it is often blurry, and outside and inside are often fused. Thus, gender socialization before entering higher education and professional life can affect the behaviors of men and women in science and engineering, and can lead them to behave in ways that run counter to Mertonian norms. In addition, the structural characteristics of training and careers, especially mentoring and networks, because they cannot work completely through formal rules, will almost inevitably reflect gender values from the broader society. McIlwee and Robinson suggest this is also true where workplace organizational structures are informal. Thus, much of the research on which I have drawn implies that the institutionalization of formal practices and procedures may improve the training and career experiences of women in science and engineering. In addition, however, Smith-Doerr's findings and clear evidence of the inevitable need for informal practices suggests that self-conscious and concerted efforts to remake the culture of science and engineering may also work to improve the experience of women in that realm.

I concluded the chapter by illustrating that gendering extends beyond the training and career experiences of scientists and engineers. This politics, however, plays itself out in an array of other technoscience-related arenas. From artifacts to the substance of research, gender affects technoscience. Technoscience is not immune from the gendered character of our social world. Indeed, gendering is one more way in which technoscience is fundamentally social.

NOTES

1   Merton's conceptualization has been roundly criticized. Mulkay (1980), for example, contends that it is not reasonable to assume that any given norm has a single literal meaning. Scientists interpret the norms Merton characterizes differently depending on the specific context within which they find themselves. Similarly, Mitroff (1974) contends that the norms that Merton describes are balanced by counternorms. Thus, the norm of communism is balanced by the counternorm of secrecy. See also Kleinman (2003: 177n18).

7

Democracy and Expertise: Citizenship in a High-Tech Age

With industrialization and the rise of the city in the nineteenth century came increased social complexity and the associated elaboration of a division of labor (Haskell 1984: xii). In such an environment one must rely on the knowledge of others. We cannot all fix our own automobiles, grow our own food, or treat our children's illnesses. We specialize. We must, in short, trust those with expert knowledge (Haskell 1984: xi; Yearly 2000; Shapin 1994). And with exceptions, trust in experts marked the modus operandi of the twentieth century, as society became increasingly complex and science and technology became increasingly central.

But the matter of trust is not a simple as it might seem. What does it mean to trust experts on science and technology-related matters if the practices and products of science and engineering are fundamentally shaped by social values and the distribution of social power? The matter of trusting experts is further complicated because if the actual practices of and artifacts produced and evaluated by experts are not neutral, neither are the experts themselves. Our experts are not free-floating specialists who are immune from social influences. Instead, we live in world in which experts are integrally part of the most powerful institutions in our society. Their orientations are shaped by their institutional affiliations. Thus, the question is not whether to trust the "truthfulness" of experts. Although surely fraud among experts occurs, this should not be our central concern. Generally, professional boards and the like provide us protection from such malfeasance. Instead, given the social nature of science, technology, and expertise, experts's assessments and decisions will inevitably reflect their social location and may not reflect the interests and concerns of non-expert citizens who are likely to be affected by experts's judgments. Recall my discussion of the partiality of knowledge in chapter 1. All knowledge reflects a perspective. It amounts to a slice from an infinite reality, and very often experts are not at all conscious of the partial character of their knowledge.

Where does this state of affairs leave us? First, to say that knowledge is fundamentally social is not to deny that it is real or, more pointedly, real in its effects. Not just any knowledge will do in solving highly technical problems of crucial social importance. The issue is deciding what knowledge is necessary and how it should be acquired and used. Second, to say that experts's perspectives reflect their social positioning is not to say that expert knowledge is not valuable. Once again, however, it is to suggest that expert knowledge is partial, not comprehensive (Haraway 1988; Harding 1986). The quality of decisions made on highly technical matters might very well be improved by broadening the array of knowledge producers beyond traditional experts. Indeed, I will argue below that the distinct vantage-point of lay people with and sometimes without a vested interest in a particular technical matter can sometimes improve the quality of related decision-making. Finally, there is inevitably a tension between democratic practice and expert decision-making. The question is how to balance these distinct modes of control and deliberation. I will suggest below that in matters where lay people have a stake in the outcome of technical decisions they are entitled to input. The question is the kind of input that is appropriate, and I will also consider this issue below.

In keeping with this assessment, the remainder of this chapter is divided into four major sections. First, I will draw on several case studies to illustrate the partial character of experts's knowledge on matters of crucial importance to specific communities. These cases highlight the limits of expert knowledge. Second, I will use these cases and several others to show how the knowledge of people who are not certified experts can improve the quality of understanding on some technical matters. Third, I will point to several cases that suggest that arguments of lay incompetence are not valid justifications for excluding non-experts from technical decision-making. Instead, in the final section of the chapter, I point to what I believe are more important barriers to lay understanding, and suggest ways in which these barriers might be surmounted.

THE LIMITS TO EXPERT KNOWLEDGE

Our commonsense view of scientists is aptly captured by Donna Haraway's term "god trick" (1988). As I noted in chapter 1, the god trick is the ability to see everything from nowhere. The idea here is that scientists are capable of a comprehensive picture of any phenomena they study and that the representation they capture does not reflect the position from which it is acquired. It does not reflect the position or perspective of the scientist. It is neutral, unbiased, and value free. Holding such a viewpoint depends on the ability to see a phenomenon from every perspective at once. It depends on the capacity of finite beings to understand any phenomena – all of which are ultimately infinitely complex – like a god might. The absurdity of such an idea makes clear the bounded nature of expert knowledge. Experts, like other human beings, see phenomena from a partial perspective. The nature of this partiality can never be neutral, unbiased, or value free, as it will always reflect, to some degree, the factors – professional socialization, institutional affiliation, and so on – that define the finitude of experts. Let me turn to several cases that illustrate this.

Investigations by epidemiologists are often relevant to the daily lives of lay people, and controversies erupting between epidemiologists and members of residential communities point to the limits of expert knowledge and the contributions lay people can make. As distinguished from work that studies health and disease in individual patients, epidemiologists investigate health and disease in populations (see Wing 2000). Populations, in this context, are understood as collections of individuals who are categorized in terms of their exposure to some possible disease agent and/or the presence or absence of the disease of concern. Studies by epidemiologists are typically based on statistical models that mimic randomized experimental design. According to one analyst, disease agent exposure measurement is often determined by "convenience, availability of data or convention, rather than based on biological models of disease process" (Wing 2000: 32). Furthermore, although exposure–disease relationships are embedded in social contexts, the messiness of including such matters in epidemiological modeling often prompts analysts's commitment to narrowly biomedical approaches.

A case in Woburn, Massachusetts, some years back points clearly to the limits of traditional epidemiological approaches (See Brown & Mikkelsen 1990 and Brown 2000). In the early 1970s, community residents noted an unusually high number of leukemia cases in Woburn. For years, residents raised concerns about foul tasting and smelling water as well as discoloration in sinks and dishwashers. By the mid-1970s, some residents believed, and had begun to investigate the possibility, that poisons in the local water supply explained an apparent leukemia cluster in their community. It was not until 1980 that government officials formally investigated the possibilities of a water–disease relationship. A joint Federal–Massachusetts investigation turned up 12 cases of childhood leukemia in East Woburn where chance alone would explain just over 5 cases. According to the Massachusetts Department of Public Health, however, the case control method in which there were 12 cases and 24 control cases did not reveal characteristics that systematically distinguished those residents with leukemia from those without. And the experts were unable to explore the linkage between water quality and disease, since they did not have environmental data for years prior to 1979. In this context, government officials and experts denied a link between water-based toxins and disease.

The limits to the assessments provided by experts in this case do not reflect malfeasance, and there is certainly no evidence to suggest that the relative inattention to the toxic chemicals ultimately found in the water and dumped by local corporations reflects some prior industry bias on the part of the involved epidemiologists. Instead, the nature of the methods used by the government-affiliated epidemiologists proved crucial. Unable to find systematic differences between study subjects with the disease and those without, scientists found no specific cause for the disease cases. Importantly, the dimensions along which cases were compared were limited by the characteristics for which the researchers had data. Scientists lacked data on water pollution, and consequently, could not rule out water as a causal agent.

The willingness of experts in this case to allow the status quo to stand reflects their professional preference for conclusions based on false negative over false positive results. Professionally, a false negative can lead a scientist to miss an important discovery. A false positive by contrast can hurt an investigator's professional reputation, possibly suggesting that her work is not sufficiently careful. Community members living in the presence of a disease cluster, by contrast, would obviously prefer to err on the side of caution. Concluding incorrectly that there is an environmental cause for a disease affecting their community will not hurt community members, but failing to recognize an environmental factor causing a disease will have important health costs for the community.

The different character of the partial perspectives of epidemiologists and community residents reflects their different social locations. In the context of their scientific investigations, epidemiologists are defined centrally by their professional identities and their employers. Professional identities define the way in which they do their research, what counts as evidence for them, and the conclusions they are willing to draw based on the evidence they have. The perspective of community residents is no less partial, but reflects a very different social location. We can see this clearly in terms of the different kinds of errors epidemiologists and community residents find acceptable. The different approaches to the research itself also illustrate the relationship between the partiality of perspective and social location. In describing the research undertaken by epidemiologists in Woburn, I noted that they could not find systematic differences between those with the disease and those without. But they were limited to those characteristics for which they had data. By contrast, living in a specific community can give residents access to information about themselves and their environment that experts simply lack. In Woburn, residents ultimately collaborated with bio-statisticians at Harvard in undertaking a resident survey. In this collaboration, residents were able to point scientists to issues that they would not have otherwise explored and also helped Harvard researchers develop survey-question wording attentive to local language and thus more likely to yield valid results. This study, along with additional water tests, led officials to accept a link between water and cancer.

Another important case that nicely illustrates the limits of expert knowledge concerns radioactive contamination on farms in England after the 1986 nuclear accident at the Chernobyl nuclear power plant in the former Soviet Union (see Wynne 1992). Initially, scientists concluded that British farms would not be affected by the cesium fallout from Chernobyl. Ultimately, however, the British government imposed far-reaching restrictions on the sale of livestock. Easing fears among sheep farmers in Cumbria that their livelihoods would be adversely affected, the government initially said the ban would last only three weeks. Government scientists asserted that the levels of radioactivity in lambs would come down below dangerous levels during that period. But instead of lifting restrictions, they were imposed indefinitely. Although only for a portion of the area initially covered by the ban, this situation created the possibility of economic devastation for area farmers.

Scientists's miscalculation of the period it would take for the levels of cesium to fall was based on an inadequate understanding of the local conditions. According to Brian Wynne, the model used by scientists was "Drawn from empirical observation of alkaline clay soils, in which cesium is chemically absorbed and immobilized and so is unable to pass into vegetation." In this case, sheep might have been affected by the fallout initially, but they would not have repeatedly consumed contaminated plants. Cumbria, however, is characterized by peaty soil, not alkaline clay soils. Thus, as Wynne observes, "scientists unwittingly transferred knowledge of the clay soils to acid peaty soil, in which cesium remains chemically mobile and available to be taken up by plant roots" (1992: 286), and consequently, sheep continued to ingest contaminated vegetation.

Scientists in this case, like the Woburn epidemiology case, knew something, but they did not know everything. Their perspective was partial, but their modeling was based "on supposed universal generalizations and universalistic principles" (Yearley 2000: 106). They were inattentive to the local environment, and knowledge of this environment is where local farmers had expertise. Farmers understood local hill characteristics, grazing, and farm management practices.

The effects of the universal orientation taken by scientists is made clear by one particular experiment. The experiment was set up to test the absorption of cesium in soil and vegetation and involved keeping sheep in fenced plots. Farmers noted that local sheep are used to roaming and would lose muscle condition in pens. Scientists ignored farmers's concerns that an experiment of this variety would not adequately model real conditions. Farmers's views ultimately won they day, when scientists abandoned the experiment because, as a result of penning, they realized it would not provide accurate results.

A final case that points to the very different perspectives experts and lay people can have, and to the bounded nature of knowledge – be that of certified experts or non-experts (see Irwin 1995) – involves an agricultural chemical. In the 1980s, the safety of the herbicide known as 2,4,5-T became an issue in Britain, pitting regulators against farmers. 2,4,5-T was used as a defoliant during the Vietnam War and has been used by homeowners, railway employees, farmers, and forestry workers to control weeds. A British government review of the scientific literature concluded that this herbicide is safe, if used according to manufacturers's recommendations and if following recommended procedures. Government conclusions about safety were based on laboratory experiments undertaken under controlled conditions. However, the National Union of Agricultural and Allied Workers in Britain argued that local circumstances often do not mirror laboratory conditions, and consequently, the union claimed that regulatory policy should not be based on pure experiments alone. To take but one issue, experiments on such chemicals typically do not model the process by which a worker might bring home chemical residues on her or his clothes which could then expose the worker's children, partner, or spouse. More generally, such laboratory experiments do not account for "all of the particularities, unusual circumstances or chance occurrences typically encountered in a normal work environment" (Crouch & Kroll-Smith 2000).

In light of member concerns, the National Union of Agricultural and Allied Workers conducted a survey of its members to ascertain worker knowledge of the use of 2,4,5-T. Broadly speaking, the conclusion of the union was that if workers lived in a world that mimicked the purity of the laboratory experiment, then it might make sense to permit use of 2,4,5-T. However, in the absence of the ability to control for all contingencies and chance events, the union argued that the chemical is likely to be dangerous, and its use should be prohibited.

These three cases each point to the partial character of expert knowledge. To say that expert knowledge is limited is not to disparage it, but to suggest that, in some cases, it is not prudent to place our trust *exclusively* in expert knowledge. When matters of broad social concern are at stake, it makes sense to systematically probe the limits of expert knowledge and to ascertain how best to supplement it and compensate for its limitations. I would suggest that in some cases, this is likely to involve lay/expert cooperation and collaboration.

The Virtues of Lay Knowledge

Beyond illustrating the limitations of expert knowledge, the three cases I discuss above, along with a host of others, also point to the contributions lay people can make in decision-making realms where it is widely assumed we should rely solely on the views of experts. Phil Brown (2000) nicely summarizes the kinds of contributions lay people can make to technical knowledge production. First, lay people – citizens with a vested interest in research on a particular topic – can root out "bad science." In the three cases above, the work of lay people showed the dangers of uncritical generalizing and of using universal models as well as the importance of recognizing the difference between laboratory and field conditions. Second, as in the Woburn and the 2,4,5-T cases, lay people can challenge the appropriateness of expert-accepted standards of proof, when human health is at risk. Finally, all three cases illustrate the ways in which lay people can sometimes provide access to important data that, without their input, would not be included in expert-based inquiry.

An array of cases beyond those I have discussed illustrate the kinds of contributions lay people can make to inquiries in which experts are often exclusively relied on. Let me turn first to the case of AIDS treatment activism in the United States. AIDS activists have been involved in practices traditionally restricted to certified scientists (designing experiments, collecting data, etc.), sometimes with the cooperation of scientists and sometimes not. In addition, activists have sometimes prevailed in arguments with scientists that the technical and nontechnical – here the scientific and the ethical – are not easily separated.

By the mid-1980s, AIDS activists were becoming increasingly frustrated by the rate of approval of experimental AIDS treatments and the "pace and scope of mainstream research" (Indyk & Rier 1993: 6; see also Epstein 1995). They became vocal in their criticisms of traditional clinical research. In one instance, activists argued that use of placebos in the Phase II AZT trial was ethically questionable since "in order to be successful the study required that a sufficient number of patients die: only by pointing to deaths in the placebo group could researchers establish that those receiving the active treatment did comparatively better" (Epstein 1996: 202). As an alternative to this protocol, activists recommended comparing treatment groups with medical records of matched cohorts of other AIDS patients or comparing patients in the treatment group with their own medical records from the period before the trial. These kinds of practices had been used in clinical trials in other areas of biomedicine.

Activists's criticisms went beyond the questionable ethics of using placebos. Activists asserted that clinical subjects concerned about receiving the placebo would find means of obtaining the drug being tested, and consequently the "purity" of the control would be undermined. Activists's insights into the kind of trials that would gain the support of people with HIV and AIDS gained the respect of many researchers – biostatisticians in particular – and led activists to have an increasingly important role in discussions about clinical trial design (Epstein 1996: 249). It was activists's local knowledge and immediate and often very personal investments in AIDS treatment that provided the basis for their contributions.

Beyond pushing for changes in research protocols, treatment activists work with community medical professionals to design community-based drug trials.[1] Following in a tradition established in cancer research, the County Community Consortium in the San Francisco area gradually became a mechanism for organizing community-based trials. As Epstein relates: "The idea was that physicians would distribute drugs, monitor patients, and collect data as an integral part of their regular clinical work with patients" (1996: 216, 217).

The work of the Community Research Initiative in New York represents a distinct variant of a community trials model. In this program, people with AIDS or HIV infection participated in decision-making about which trials should be conducted and how they should be designed. Drug companies became interested in CRI and signed several contracts with the group to undertake community-based studies (Epstein 1996: 217). Significantly, the US Food and Drug Administration (FDA) relied on data collected in Community Research Initiative (CRI) and County Community Consortium trials in deciding to approve the drug pentamidine. The commissioner of the FDA praised the CRI trial model. This model has since been used in some trials sponsored by the US National Institutes of Health. Significantly, however, this was the first time in the agency's history that it had approved a drug based solely on data from community-based trials (Epstein 1996: 218).

Central to the success of AIDS treatment activists has been the acquisition of a working knowledge of the language and culture of medical science (Epstein 1995: 417). Many of these activists started with little background in science, but managed to learn the rudiments of AIDS-related biomedicine. Often this involved attending scientific conferences, scrutinizing research protocols, and learning from sympathetic professionals.

Treatment activists have been successful in challenging the notion that only certified experts can engage in the day-to-day research practices of biomedical science. Their experience provides evidence that it is possible to become conversant in the mode of reasoning and the language of clinical practice without becoming a certified scientist. These activists have argued, furthermore, that it is problematic to sharply divide the technical (research methods) from the nontechnical (questions of ethics), and they have shown that paying attention to the blurred boundary between the two can lead to "better science." As Epstein notes, however, the successes of AIDS treatment activists may have unintended consequences as well. As one example, he describes a scenario in which researchers are unable to recruit subjects for postmarket studies to assess a drug's efficacy, because potential users believe that FDA's accelerated approval, for which activists pushed, indicates the drug is effective (1996: 344).

A second case that illustrates the kinds of contributions lay participants can make to technical discussions or disputes is reflected in the work of a grassroots group called the Endometriosis Association (EA). This organization was founded in 1980 by women who had the disease, and their work has played a significant role in recasting the way in which medical professionals think about endometriosis (see Capek 2000). Endometriosis is a disease in which tissue like the endometrium, which lines a woman's uterus, is found outside the uterus. These growths can cause an array of problems, including pain and infertility. Prior to the founding of the Endometriosis Association, the medical profession understood endometriosis primarily as a reproductive or fertility disease. According to one analyst of the EA, historically, understanding of the disease has been shaped by gender biases (Capek 2000: 348). It is sometimes called the "career woman's disease," and for many years medical professionals assumed that endometriosis affected primarily white and well-educated career women. As a result, doctors often recommended childbirth as the a cure for the disease. Another treatment often recommended was hysterectomy. One study went so far as to conclude that the origins of the disease could be found in women's "rejection of femininity," and some doctors viewed the roots of the disease as fundamentally individual and psychological (Capek 2000: 349).

Unhappy with what appeared to them to be inadequate research on the disease and social bias in diagnosis, the women who formed the EA came together to enhance understanding of the disease. Working with the medical profession, since its founding the EA has sought to challenge traditional views of the disease and has promoted innovative research. The organization has never been antiscience, but has sought to challenge cultural biases that organization members believed may have hindered understanding of endometriosis. The EA created a disease registry to collect data about women with the disease. That registry revealed "that endometriosis often affects very young adolescents, that it affects women of all races and income groups in various stages of their lives, that having a baby or a hysterectomy is not necessarily a cure, and that it is a global problem" (Capek 2000: 349, 350). In short, the data in the registry challenged the narrow notion that the disease affects primarily white career women and that the traditional cures are typically appropriate.

Beyond challenging the demographic profile of those with the disease and the appropriateness of traditional treatments, registry data suggested that endometriosis is a immunological disease with reproductive and immunological symptoms (Capek 2000: 352). This picture was reinforced by a study of rhesus monkeys supported by the association. This work, undertaken at the University of Wisconsin–Madison, revealed that 79 percent of monkeys exposed to dioxin had endometrial growths outside their uteruses. The study also found a correlation between dioxin level and severity of disease (Capek 2000: 353).

Through highlighting their individual and personal knowledge and searching out new information, members of the EA successfully challenged existing assumptions about endometriosis. The work of the organization provided support for the idea that the source of endometriosis is not narrowly physiological, but appears to have environmental and hence social sources. Members of the EA had personal investments in understanding the disease, and their individual experiences and the data they gathered led them to challenge biases held by experts. The work of the EA illustrates the importance of "a bottom-up flow of knowledge, grounded in the practical, daily lived experiences of ordinary citizens" (Capek 2000: 346). It does not suggest that lay people must or should pursue their investigations independent of experts. Instead, it shows that scientists, working with lay citizens with endometriosis, are in a better position to understand the disease. At a general level, we can say that this case, like the cases of popular epidemiology and AIDS treatment activism, suggests that participatory initiatives and lay understanding can produce better science and consequently better expert decisions.

One of the central contributions made by some varieties of lay participation in expert realms is the inclusion of considerations beyond the narrowly technical in efforts to understand the phenomena of concern. This is true in the way AIDS treatment activists fused questions of the ethics of placebos with practical concerns about the workability of clinical trials that rely on placebo use. But the virtues of moving beyond the relatively narrow concerns of traditionally trained technical experts is even more clear in the efforts of the Endometriosis Association and popular epidemiology activists. Importantly, in both cases, lay people pushed for an analysis of disease that considered factors beyond individual genetics and physiology and called for attention to what might be broadly termed social factors. By turning attention to immunological factors in the etiology of endometriosis, the EA focused attention not just on environmental factors, but more crucially, if implicitly, on the producers of dioxin and the social organization of the economy that has led to the saturation of the environment with industrial pollutants. Likewise, popular epidemiology – lay citizen involvement in epidemiological research – is more explicitly attentive, than traditional science, to the role of social structural factors in explaining disease (Brown & Mikkelsen 1990: 126). Thus, lay citizens engaged in popular epidemiology are more likely than certified epidemiologists to explore to factors of politics and economy, like incentives or disincentives for corporate pollution and the intimate relationships that sometimes exist between government regulators and regulated corporations.

Outside the cases of what might be termed biomedical activism, a distinctive mechanism for broadening the factors trained experts are likely to consider in highly technical matters are so-called consensus conferences. Pioneered in Denmark in the late 1980s, these fora involve lay people in deliberation over technical matters of concern not to scientists but to policymakers. The involved lay people typically do not share the stakeholder investments of Woburn citizens AIDS treatment activists, or EA members, and they are not directly and explicitly involved in the production of technical knowledge. Instead, these citizens focus on science and technology policy-related issues. But like the other cases I have considered, consensus conferences are likely to extend discussion beyond the topics typically contemplated by trained experts.

Consensus conferences have been utilized in a number of countries, and although they are roughly similar in their mode of operation, exhibit notable variation. Topics covered by consensus conferences have ranged from the future of private automobiles to the relationship of telecommunications and democracy to biotechnology in agriculture.

In Denmark, topics are selected on the basis of their broad social and legislative importance, and drawing conclusions demands that conference participants examine diverse dimensions of the issue under consideration. With a topic chosen, the Board advertises for volunteer lay participants who provide written statements of interest and are selected to ensure representation of the social diversity of the nation. Participants have access to information from commissioned expert background papers, meetings with "expert panels" representing a wide range of viewpoints, and public fora. Ultimately, the group meets to draw conclusions on the basis of the information it has reviewed.

There is some question about how influential such panels are in shaping policy or in guiding technological development (Guston 1999), but there is little question that this mechanism for deliberation broadens discussion. In a comparison of consensus conferences on food biotechnology conducted in Denmark, Canada, and Australia, Einsiedel, Jelsøe, and Breck (2001) found that lay members of these fora framed their discussion very broadly, considering the social organization the food system, raising issues of corporate control of agriculture and the impacts of current production practices on the third world, farming communities, and animal welfare. As Einsiedel, Jelsøe, and Breck put it, the final documents produced by these consensus conferences challenge the narrow "technical tropes of scientific risk discourse" (2000: 94). They note that

Such a discourse, which characterizes the regulatory approach in many industrialized countries and which . . . almost invariably carries the messages that genetically modified food is "unequivocally" safe to eat, is environmentally benign, and comes with a fully array of benefits . . . was shown by all three panels to be inadequate if not flawed. On the contrary, all three panels discuss risk in broader terms, encompassing uncertainties and unknown effects as well as long term consequences. (2000: 94, 95)

From the Endometriosis Association to AIDS treatment activism to consensus conferences, we see that lay people can contribute to discussions generally restricted to experts. We see, furthermore, that lay people can broaden the range of these discussions and sometimes contribute to the production of technical knowledge and thereby improve expert practice.

BARRIERS TO DEMOCRATIZING TECHNOSCIENCE AND EXPERTISE[2]

The central argument made against lay participation in decisions traditionally left to experts is that many lay people are scientifically illiterate (Levitt & Gross 1994). Illiteracy, in this context, is understood to mean that lay people are ignorant of scientific facts. As Yearly notes, however, data on scientific literacy comes from surveys that are fundamentally flawed:

The survey quiz questions used to estimate the public's understanding of science ask about more or less context-free science. . . . But in everyday situations people have to use scientific information in a context-sensitive way. And this difference is what makes the usual attempts to assess the public understanding of science through quiz-type questions unrealistic. (2000: 226)

In contrast to data from these types of surveys, an interactive exercise from the early 1990s in which lay people discussed technical matters showed that "people who do not ordinarily keep abreast of scientific issues can quickly learn about their crucial aspects" (Doble & Richardson 1992: 52). And a slew of case studies shows that lay people are "very capable of acquiring scientific knowledge and responding to the demands of technical debate when they are highly motivated to do so" (Yearly 2000: 228). What is more, the knowledge of citizens in these situations is not of the context-free variety that is assessed in scientific literacy surveys, but is instead of a context-sensitive type that involves understanding what are traditionally viewed as the technical matters at stake in relationship to institutional context. Citizens are motivated to understand the "facts" in relationship to who the actors participating in a given controversy are, what interests they bring to the table, and how these actors's interests affect their understandings of the "facts."

The cases I discuss above support this assessment. Members of the Endometriosis Association, for example, did not stop with understanding existing data on the causes of the disease, but explored how gender and cultural biases may have affected where scientists looked to find the causes of the disease. Similarly, in the Woburn case, citizens were attentive to how the relationship between industry and government affected the way in which epidemiologists studied the possible cancer clusters in their community. In addition, biostatisticians in this case ultimately acknowledged that the knowledge of Woburn residents allowed them to do better science than they would have otherwise been able to do. Finally, analysts of consensus conferences believe that participants show themselves more than capable of understanding the technical issues at stake, and furthermore promote context-sensitive discussion of these issues.

Against those who bemoan lay ignorance and incapacity on technical matters, the case of AIDS treatment activism is perhaps the strongest example I profile of lay understanding. Importantly in this instance, although they were initially doubtful that the activists could participate intelligently in discussions about AIDS-related bioscience, the activists proved the scientists wrong. According to Steven Epstein, able to speak the language of biomedicine, activists "increasingly discovered that researchers felt compelled, by their own norms of discourse and behavior, to consider activist arguments on their merits" (Epstein 1995: 419; 1996: 230–2).

Even if lay people are potentially capable of intelligent participation in matters often restricted to experts, the barriers to truly democratized science and technology are formidable. These barriers are part and parcel of the organization of the society in which we live. It is a society characterized by wide-ranging varieties of social and economic inequality and inequity, and dominated by the widespread belief in the superior judgment of certified experts. Within this context, citizen participation will often be constrained by the free time (Krimsky 1984b: 48; Elster 1998) and economic resources to which citizens have access (Nelkin 1984: 34). In addition, in deliberative bodies composed of lay citizens, social dynamics rooted in such forces as gender inequality are likely to mar the deliberative process (Bohman 1996).

An important case illustrating these kinds of barriers involves the Cambridge Laboratory Experimentation Review Board (CERB). The board was created in 1976 by the Cambridge, Massachusetts, city manager to explore regulation of recombinant DNA research going on at universities within the city's limits. Members's occupations included: structural engineer, physician, philosopher of science, nurse/hospital administrator, nurse/social worker, community activist, former city councilor, and a businessperson who was formerly mayor. Before issuing a report, the board spent approximately 100 hours in session over 4 months, hearing testimony from proponents and opponents of rDNA research and studying the matter collectively. In addition, members read an array of materials in order to reach an understanding of the issues at stake.

In terms of the limitations of the process, board members accepted the narrowly defined contours of their charge. Following traditional views of expertise (cf. Goggin 1986b: 264; Kleinman & Kloppenburg 1991), they accepted the sharp distinction between clearly technical and nontechnical issues. They dealt only with the issues surrounding the safety of various genetically engineered organisms and the appropriate physical structures for containing them. What board members and observers understood as ethical and social issues were excluded from formal discussion. Making this sharp distinction was precisely the way in which leading scientists in the field hoped the issue would be handled. Biologist and active genetic engineering debate participant David Baltimore, for example, talked about leaving questions "replete with value and political motivations" out of the discussion (quoted in Krimsky 1982: 106). This suggests that there is some realm that is free of value and political motivations. But certainly the decision to restrict the discussion is itself "replete with value and political motivations." What is more, the matters on which the board ultimately focused – acceptable levels of risk and the balancing of risks and benefits – must inevitably be value-laden (see Krimsky 1986b).

In addition to accepting the terms of debate as defined by scientists, the establishment of the CERB reinforced rather than challenged the notion of expertise itself. The board listened almost exclusively to the testimony of certified experts. This procedural decision could certainly have shaped the findings of the board, but in addition, in their own thinking, board members did not escape the commonly accepted notions of expertise. Importantly, as board members acknowledged, their decisions were not only influenced by the *substance* of what testifying experts said, but also in important ways by the experts's *credentials* (Goodell 1979: 40).

Within the board itself a power dynamic mirrored those existing in the broader society. The Cambridge city manager selected board members in part on the basis of their own expertise. Thus, the Board medical professionals could, in theory, speak to issues of health hazard and the engineer could evaluate the structural efficacy of proposed containment facilities. This decision was reinforced by board members's own attitudes toward other board members. Board members took for granted the legitimacy of generally accepted boundaries between lay and expert realms and granted traditionally defined experts privileged status. According to one analyst of the body's history, the confidence of board members varied enormously, "ranging from two physicians who quickly became vocal proponents of the research, and . . . a philosopher of science from Tufts who played 'devils advocate,' to a nurse and a nun who hardly spoke at all." Everyone on the CERB, according to this analyst, "looked to the two physicians for arbitration of technical difficulties and to the [philosopher] . . . to find any chinks in their armor" (Goodell 1979: 13). In his own discussion of the board, one former board member implies that the powerful influence of the "medical people on the committee was justified by their knowledge" (Krimsky 1982: 302). Here, this member seems to be taking for granted the appropriateness of the social status of the medical profession and ignoring the possibility that even an expert's evaluation of information *may* be affected by an array of interests (e.g. in the unambiguous benefits of scientific research), beliefs (e.g. the relative infallibility of doctors), and values (e.g. the appropriate balance between risk and benefit). In addition, the internal dynamic of the committee may not have been exclusively shaped by the social status granted experts. Research suggests that the most vocal board members were men, and the women spoke rarely. Thus, a gender dynamic may have been at work.

Truly open and hence democratic debate was hindered in the Cambridge case by two other factors. First, no effort was made by those with knowledge considered relevant to the committee's charge to systematically share that knowledge with others on the committee (Krimsky 1982: 302). Second, as one student of the CERB discovered, certified experts who were critical of the plan to build an rDNA laboratory at Harvard or critical of genetic engineering research more generally "were reluctant to testify in opposition to colleagues, friends, and superiors and fearful of social and professional alienation" (Goodell 1979: 83). In short, if democratic deliberation depends on the unimpeded flow of information and free and open discussion (see Bohman 1996), the CERB case provides ample examples of distortion of democracy in action.

To suggest that lay persons acknowledged the expert qualifications of some persons and unquestioningly accepted the validity of their claims on that account is not to suggest that the word of experts must inevitably be rejected. As I noted in the introduction to this chapter, complex societies's trust in experts is crucial to their functioning. More broadly, Steven Shapin's work (1994) makes clear that *trust* is the foundation on which knowledge exists. We must rely on the "word" of others. In securing knowledge, Shapin suggests, "we rely upon others, and we cannot dispense with that reliance. That means that the relations in which we have and hold our knowledge have a moral character." Trust is the word that indicates that moral relation (Shapin 1994: xxv). Thus, we can only have reliable knowledge to the extent that the people on whom we rely are "reputable and veracious sources, and act appropriately with respect to their testimony" (Shapin 1994: 9).

In the case of scientists, we are asked to trust the institution which they represent and to do so because the norms which govern it are said to stifle regular transgression. But, as I have suggested, simple and clear normative transgression is not the problem. In antiquity, "One's word was one's bond only if one was not bound in giving it. The forgoing of free action was considered effective and reliable only if that course was freely decided upon" (Shapin 1994: 39). In the cases I have discussed, blanket acquiescence is problematic not because self-policing is inadequate, but because in a world of institutions one's "word" is never "freely" given. As my discussions of the Woburn case, the Endometriosis Association, and AIDS treatment activism suggest, what counts as a significant finding and what constitutes a legitimate research protocol are shaped by specific institutional histories and social biases and, indeed, reinforced by the very norms which are supposed to provide the basis for lay confidence in scientists's words.

Of course, the costs of consistent and unrelenting skepticism would make social life unbearably difficult. Certainly, most of the time unexamined trust is practically appropriate. But where the stake of one's community, family, or person is at issue, some measure of skepticism may be healthy. Prodding one's doctor about a diagnosis and seeking a second and perhaps third opinion seems entirely reasonable behavior. It is no less the case that citizens should not assume that the way experts frame a problem or interpret data is valid and appropriate merely because of the credentials the expert holds.

The case of AIDS treatment activism illustrates a different way in which the politics of expertise and the power dynamics that constitute social relations in the United States can affect efforts to include lay people in the practice and regulation of technoscience. The social status of economically well-off gay white men who composed the core of the AIDS treatment activism movement has provided the foundation for the respect they have been granted by AIDS medical professionals, and among their "constituency" (Epstein 1996: 294). As the demographics of AIDS changes and the growth of AIDS slows among the middle-income gay population, while increasing among IV drug users and people of color, it is unlikely that these latter groups will have the same capacity that gay white men have had to enter the world of biomedicine (Epstein 1995; 1991).

Furthermore, with so few people in the position to become successful treatment activists – in part because they lack time, economic resources, and social status – there is every likelihood that the treatment movement will reproduce within the community of people with AIDS or more narrowly the AIDS activist community the lay/expert dynamic which exists in society at large (Epstein 1991: 52, 53, 60; 1996: 294). There will be those few who are in a position to enter the "halls of science" and those who must depend on movement activists for information, advice, and representation. Indeed, Epstein suggests that this is already occurring (Epstein 1996: 288). Of course, as other analysts have noted (Indyk & Rier 1991: 11; Epstein 1995), the question of representation – closely related to the problem of democracy – raises the important issue of whether middle-class, gay white men represent all people with AIDS in any case or only activists. Women and people of color in the AIDS treatment activism movement have been critical of treatment activist leaders for their inattention to issues of concern to "minority" communities among people with AIDS or HIV disease (Epstein 1996: 291).[3]

STRATEGIES FOR OVERCOMING THE OBSTACLES

The obstacles to democratizing science within the existing social order are formidable, and some may be ultimately insurmountable. But while the barriers are unlikely to be entirely transcended, there are a range of possible strategies that would enhance the likelihood that these obstacles can be at least partially surmounted and the quality of outcomes from efforts to democratize science be enhanced.

Instances of working-class citizen participation in popular epidemiology notwithstanding, lack of resources is an important barrier to broad social representation in efforts to democratize science, from consensus conferences and popular epidemiology to AIDS treatment activism. One must be able to afford time away from work and family to participate, and the resource requirement will be significantly greater in cases in which broad technical mastery is necessary (like AIDS treatment activism) in contrast to cases in which citizens must simply attend to the testimony of certified experts and other stakeholders (like consensus conferences).

Participation in juries in civil and criminal trials is widely considered a responsibility of citizenship in the United States, and jurors are granted a per diem. Federal advisory panels similarly offer payment for daily expenses. For jury service, the payment offered is plainly inadequate compensation. The idea, however, is important. For the array of citizen bodies that provide advice to governments, economic leaders, and the public at large, including community boards and experiments with consensus conferences, some type of per diem system could weaken economic barriers to widespread citizen participation. Where fiscal constraints make government contributions to such a system impossible, support from private foundations with a commitment to democracy and public understanding of public policy and socially relevant science and technology might be sought. Cases like the Endometriosis Association, the Woburn popular epidemiology effort, and the work of AIDS treatment activists require a greater commitment of citizen time and are consequently more costly.

As a way of enhancing citizens's "appreciation of the diverse needs of other communities, [and providing them] a broader experiential basis from which to conceive of their society's general interest," Richard Sclove has proposed "citizen sabbaticals." Sclove views these as analogous to faculty sabbaticals or the US Peace Corps. Such sabbaticals would "encourage each person to occasionally take a leave of absence from his or her home community, to live and work for perhaps a month each year or a year each decade in another community, culture, or region" (1995: 43).

For the purpose of increasing lay involvement in the production and evaluation of scientific knowledge and technologies, citizen fellowships might be established along similar lines. If government funds were not available, private foundations might be in the position to establish an endowment which would provide funds to allow a limited number of citizens to take leaves of absence from their jobs in order to work for an extended period on a science-related project. Nonprofit organizations doing science- and technology-related work, for-profit companies, and government and university laboratories and science departments could list opportunities in a database compiled by the entity overseeing the endowment. Citizens would then choose one of these opportunities and submit a statement of interest. Statements would be evaluated and citizens selected by a committee including people representing diverse interests and social, economic, and professional backgrounds.

The virtue of such a program from the perspective of enhancing democratization is beyond doubt. What citizens and participating organizations would gain is certainly open to question and would vary. One can imagine, however, a case in which a farmer received such a fellowship and went to work in an agricultural biology lab on a nearby university campus. The farmer and the scientists would have an opportunity to come to know one another. Developing rapport and respect, all parties might conceivably leave the project with enhanced empathy for the others's interests and needs. In addition, however, the research subsequently produced by the lab might benefit from the synergy of the intimate knowledge of farming the farmer brought to the lab and the more traditional biological science in which the lab researchers typically work (cf. Krimsky 1984). AIDS researcher Anthony Fauci has spoken enthusiastically about the time treatment activists spent in his lab. Activists gained a better understanding of the "bench science," and researchers were forced to confront the realities of the disease. As some scientists have gratefully acknowledged, activist involvement with basic AIDS research also prompted dialogue between scientists in distinct specialties (Epstein 1996: 321, 322).

If citizen involvement in the realm of science is to be successful, work must be undertaken to institutionalize mechanisms that allow participants the opportunity to acquire the broadest possible "knowledge base," that promote reflection upon taken-for-granted attitudes toward expertise held by participants (Laird 1993: 354), and that maximize the possibility of equal roles for all participants. Two techniques used in educational settings might be utilized as a means of promoting equitable participation by lay citizens in the realm of technoscience.

First, to promote learning environments in which students are not structurally excluded from participation, a common practice is to break large lecture classes down into smaller discussion groups. These groups work for a period without monitoring by the teacher, and later each group reports back to the classroom as a whole. The advantage of such a procedure is that it can encourage students who are fearful of talking before the entire class to express their views. Perhaps a modification of such a practice could work in citizen science and technology boards.

A second technique, used sometimes in the classroom, might involve roll playing. Citizen bodies might collectively outline the range of positions possible on a given issue and then randomly assign group members to argue for each position. This approach has the advantage that group members with superior presentational and rhetorical capacities, more confidence in public speaking, and/or respect based on some credential not automatically warranting respect would not always be arguing for the positions they most favor and thereby dominating group deliberations.[4]

Trained monitors might observe group deliberations, and specific times in group meetings might be set aside for collective self-reflection. Monitors would explore group dynamics, determining who dominates discussion and trying to ascertain why. Special attention would be paid to determine whether certain positions are rejected out of hand by some participants and others are accepted without evaluation. Of course, a methodology for monitoring and assessment would need to be developed, but similar practices are undertaken in classrooms throughout the country with the aim of enhancing teacher effectiveness and prompting more equitable student participation (Sadker & Sadker 1994).

The "remedies" outlined above speak only to barriers to citizen participation in the practices of democratizing science. But, as all successful efforts in this direction – from consensus conferences to popular epidemiology and AIDS research – suggest, cooperation between scientists and lay persons is absolutely essential. From the perspective of scientists, while there may on occasion be legitimacy incentives to limited participation, as I suggested above, there may be disincentives as well. There may be little that can be formally done to protect participating scientists from colleague ostracism. However, including faculty records of cooperation with citizen groups as part of the service component considered in tenure and promotion decisions for university scientists might very well increase scientists's willingness to cooperate, and could conceivably offer them a measure of protection from hostile colleagues.

In this context, there are contemporary and historical legacies to which supporters of democratized science might look in an effort to alter university policy. Collaboration between university biologists and industry is increasingly viewed in a favorable light by academic administrators and can even enhance promotion prospects. What is more, "service," while often devalued, is formally considered in promotion decisions at most universities, and land grant universities have a long tradition of outreach to rural communities. Of course, interest in industry involvement in university science is often predicated on the money it will bring to institutions confronting fiscal hard times, and there is little financially that citizens can offer universities. On the other hand, citizens are voters, and state universities depend on legislators's kind heartedness. Indeed, seeking legislators's favor could be an incentive for university administrators to take cooperation with citizens more seriously in promotion policies, and at federal land grant institutions could be used to alter current outreach practices.

CONCLUSIONS

In this chapter I have made three general points. First, through a discussion of several different cases, I have shown the bounded or partial character of expert knowledge. Second, also through analysis of real cases, I have shown that lay people can contribute to the production of knowledge relevant to solving broadly technical problems. I have illustrated how drawing lay and expert knowledge together can produce more complete and more helpful understanding. Next, I used several instances of citizen involvement in highly technical situations to support my contention that lay people are fully capable of understanding highly technical matters, and thus, lay incompetence cannot be used to justify excluding non-experts from highly technical decision-making. Finally, I argued that the real barriers to lay participation in decision-making in matters traditionally restricted to experts stem from pervasive forms of social inequality and inequity as well as the unreflected-upon stature widely granted to experts. This situation notwithstanding, I suggested that in specific cases there may be ways to overcome these constraints.

Considering the relationship between democracy and expertise is, I think, an appropriate issue with which to conclude this book. Having illustrated the myriad ways in which science and technology are fundamentally social and political – thoroughly shaped by the world in which they are embedded – it makes sense to raise questions about what such an analysis means for choice in technoscientific practice and the role of experts and non-experts in shaping science and technology. If science and technology are social and political, experts (the creators of science and technology) must be taken off of their pedestal. The world is complicated. Clearly, we cannot do without specialists, but we must understand that they are engaged in social practices, and insofar as those practices affect a wide array of nonspecialist citizens, we must develop a set of mechanisms that allow for fruitful collaboration between specialists and interested citizens – collaboration that will produce less partial perspectives in and on science and technology and so better social choices.

NOTES

1   The efforts of the Boston Women's Health Collective, beginning in 1969, provide another compelling example of lay involvement in a realm traditionally restricted to experts. The major product of the Collective's work is *Our Bodies, Ourselves*. Since its initial publication, the book has been translated into 19 languages and has been regularly revised and updated. See www.ourbodiesourselves.org, accessed Dec. 24, 2004.

2   Parts of this section of chapter 7 and virtually all of the subsequent section appeared originally as part of my paper "Beyond the Science Wars: Science, Technology, and Democracy," *Politics and the Life Sciences* 16(2): 133–45.

3   In the recent case of whether placebo-based clinical trials should be used in testing drugs to prevent mother–child transmission of HIV in the developing world, activists took a position akin to that taken by North American AIDS treatment activists. However, the activist leadership in this case appears not to be from the affected communities in Africa, for example, but are established scientists associated with a public interest group and other established institutions in the United States, suggesting that the lay/expert dynamic in society at large has been, at least in part, reproduced in the international community of AIDS activists.

4   I have borrowed this idea from Steve Schneider, who suggested it to me in a conversation over a somewhat different matter: how to make debates over controversies among scientists equitable.

8

Confronting the Problem: A Summary and Coda

I began this book with a very basic argument. I suggested that as a society our capacity to think critically about science and technology is inhibited by two powerful discourses, *scientism* and *technological progressivism*. As I see it, there are three related dimensions to scientism. The first is the idea that facts and values are inherently separate categories of phenomena. Second, scientism suggests that facts are superior to values, and finally, this discourse grants superior cultural authority to those recognized as experts at "uncovering" facts – that is, scientists. In this context, the supreme authority we grant to science rests on the assumption that science is value-free and politically neutral. Where there is controversy, we tend to believe scientists are capable of sorting through the data to find the politically neutral truth of the matter.

The second discourse that limits our ability to think critically about science and technology is what I term technological progressivism. I argued that we have come to believe that technological developments are inherently progressive: they move us forward as a society, improving the quality of our lives. Central to this orientation to the world is the idea that technology, or at least its path of development, is fundamentally asocial. It exists somehow outside of society and is, in some fashion, self-propelling. It develops along a path immanent in the technology itself, and thus, there is just this one road. It is not socially shaped or subject to social choice.

In chapter 1 and in subsequent chapters, I showed that contrary to these discourses science and technology are simultaneously social and political. I suggested that scientific categories and orientations as well as professional practices and the very "facts" that scientists reveal are shaped in important ways by the culture in which research is undertaken, the way scientific disciplines are organized, and norms of the field into which scientists are socialized. I showed that how a given artifact develops or is utilized is shaped by an array of social and political factors. In both cases, I argued that the social organization of power matters.

Let me summarize briefly.

Chapter 2. Through case studies of herbicide-resistant crops, so-called "terminator technology," recombinant bovine growth hormone, and the transfer of genes from *Bacillus thuringiensis* (*Bt*), a common soil bacterium, to crop plants, I showed how the trajectory of the development of agricultural biotechnology has been shaped by agribusiness, and I argued that, to date and for the foreseeable future, agribusiness is likely to be the single biggest beneficiary of developments in agricultural biotechnology. At the farm level, I suggested that the primary winners in the world of agribiotechnologies have been and are likely to continue to be large-scale producers whose farm organization and orientation is consistent with well-established historical trends. Smaller enterprises that produce organic crops, for example, are likely to face ongoing struggles. In this context, I illustrated how the push of corporate profits has directed the development of agricultural biotechnology in ways that, in many cases, undermine farmer control over production processes.

Chapter 3. Among other things, I undertook an analysis of the so-called "digital divide." I suggested that the desire to overcome the digital divide reflects a kind of technological progressivism. Advocates of devoting substantial effort to eliminating the gap between the "information haves" and the "information have-nots" believe that doing so will improve the quality of life of our less fortunate citizens and broadly decrease social inequality. By contrast, I argued that the digital divide reflects deep social and economic inequalities, and I believe that without addressing these fundamental disparities, eliminating digital inequalities will do little to improve the vast economic gulf in American life.

In chapter 3, I also argued that the uncritical embrace of information technology in our education system reflects the implicit belief that all new technology is good and valuable. I showed that much use of information technology in educational settings does little to improve the quality of our students's education. I suggested that many of the crucial skills students learn in school are not necessarily instilled more effectively with computer technology than by more traditional means, and that computer-specific skills are easily and relatively quickly taught and thus need not be the center of primary or secondary school programs. Finally, I suggested that despite the praise lavished on information technology as a means of improving the democratic character of politics, our assessment should be more tempered. I showed that although information technology has created some opportunities for new forms of political action, many of the developments in computer-assisted politics have done little to deepen democracy.

Chapter 4. Our fast-moving, high-technology world is deeply shaped by our intellectual property regime. I argued that, contrary to the common wisdom, it is not at all clear that intellectual property protection promotes innovation, the primary justification for our patent and copyright systems. Exploring an array of developments in information technology and biological science, I showed that intellectual property protection trends are narrowing the knowledge commons – the social space of new ideas – and reinforcing the power of large corporations at the expense of many musicians and other artists, academic scientists, and the citizens of the global south.

Chapter 5. As in chapters 2 and 3, I suggested that central developments in science and technology reflect the social organization of the world in which they occur and, in particular, the character of widespread social inequalities. Centrally, I showed that the colonial appropriation of genetic resources from the global south was part of a larger process which undermined the economic development of that part of the world. I showed, furthermore, how current developments in bioprospecting or biopiracy are fundamentally configured by ideas about property, knowledge, and invention that generally advantage people from the global north over those from the south. Importantly, the case of genetic resources shows quite clearly that the idea of "objective" knowledge is highly problematic. Many "partial perspectives" make up our understanding of genetic resources, and the divergent values placed on these knowledges reflect the different interests and power of actors from the global north and south. Finally, I suggested that if we are interested in promoting innovations based on genetic resources in ways that will provide relatively equitable benefits to people across the globe, compensation for all parties based on the established system of intellectual property protection may not be the best means.

Chapter 6. Here, I moved away from specific technologies and the laws shaping their development and turned my attention to the gendered character of science and engineering (S&E). I focused on the divergent experiences of women and men who seek to make careers in S&E. Drawing on an extensive literature, I showed that the successes and failures of men and women in S&E cannot be primarily explained in terms of "merit" and the "quality" of their work. Instead, an array of social factors provides a considerable part of the explanation for why men tend to have more successful careers in S&E than women. Among these factors are: early gender socialization, opportunities for mentoring in graduate school, and inclusion in or exclusion from professional networks. Gender socialization affects the kinds of choices boys and girls make about careers and their comfort levels in science and engineering environments. The experiences boys have are more likely than the experiences girls have to lead them to careers in S&E and to "fit" in those careers. In university and professional settings, young female scientists and engineers are likely to be mentored less well than their male counterparts and to be less fully integrated into the networks that are likely to facilitate professional success. As I showed in previous chapters, here too the character of science and engineering as professions reflects the larger social world in which they are embedded.

Chapter 7. In this chapter I challenged the idea that developments in science and technology must inevitably be shaped by scientism and technological progressivism. I provided descriptions of several cases in which lay people – often working with experts – pushed science and technology in directions that they might not have gone left in the hands of experts and/or corporations alone. The cases I described show that lay people are fully capable of understanding highly technical matters and can often add insights to scientific and technological developments that those who traditionally have controlled science and technology would not arrive at on their own. While I outlined a number of barriers to fully democratizing technoscience, I showed that there is evidence that democratization is possible and can be socially beneficial.

Across the 7 chapters that constitute the core of this book, I have traversed some of the most important science- and technology-related issues that confront us as we move through the early twenty-first century. There is an important disjuncture between chapters 1 through 6 and chapter 7 that may not be apparent to the average reader of this volume. In all of the chapters but chapter 7, I suggested that science and technology are shaped by an array of social factors that are largely beyond the capacity of individuals to alter. In chapter 1, I argued that we live in a world shaped in fundamental ways by structures, uneven resource distributions, and dominant discourses. I suggested that structures define formal and informal, explicit and implicit "rules of play" and that together structures, resource distributions, and dominant discourses create specific constraints and opportunities for actors, often depending on their location in a structural matrix.

In the parlance of traditional social science, one might suggest that I have taken a structure-centered view of the social world, a view in which those forces that shape us are, following Emile Durkheim, external (outside the capacity of individuals to alter) and constraining. Crudely, such a perspective is often juxtaposed to an agency-centered view of the social world in which the practices, behaviors, and ideas of people are fundamentally self-shaped. From this perspective, people are active agents in the construction of their own worlds and lives. They shape and constitute the constraints with which we all live.

While I am in complete agreement with those who say this kind of dichotomy is too simple, I do believe that, broadly speaking, social forces are external and constraining on social actors. At the same time, understanding how these forces operate can change us from social dopes to more active agents. Karl Marx talked about history happening behind our backs. The more we understand social history as it unfolds, the greater our capacity to shape it. Ultimately, social (re)shaping is a collective project. It demands that people first understand the social world they inhabit and then work together to change it. The limited number of experiments in democratizing technoscience that I described in chapter 7 are meant to inspire readers. Each involved collective action of various sorts. With a deep understanding of how science and technology infuses our world, we should be better placed to shape their future development. Doing so will not be easy, but the capacity for critical examination is an important first step. In the preceding pages, I provided some tools and some substantive material for such an examination.

References

Angier, Natalie. 1988. *Natural Obsessions: The Search for the Oncogene.* New York: Houghton Mifflin.

Apple, Michael W. and Susan Jungck. 1998. " 'You Don't have to be a Teacher to Teach this Unit': Teaching, Technology, and Control in the Classroom." In Hank Bromley and Michael W. Apple (eds.), *Education/Technology/Power: Educational Computing as a Social Practice.* Albany, NY: SUNY Press.

Baber, Zaheer. 1996. *The Science of Empire: Scientific Knowledge, Civilization, and Colonial Rule in India.* Albany, NY: SUNY Press.

Barham, Bradford, Douglas Jackson-Smith, and Sunung Moon. 2001. "Use and Implications of Bovine Somatotropin for the Wisconsin Dairy Sector in the 1990s," *PATS Research Report* no. 9 (June).

Barnoff, Harvey S. 2001. "Provir Shows Benefits for AIDS-Related Diarrhea Not Due to Infection." At www.hivandhepatitis.com. Accessed Dec. 17, 2003.

Bellah, Robert. 1996. *Habits of the Heart: Individualism and Commitment in American Life,* 2nd edn. Berkeley, CA: University of California Press.

Benkler, Yochai. 2004. "Commons-Based Strategies and the Problem of Patents," *Science* 305(5687) (Aug. 20): 1110–11.

Bloor, David. 1976. *Knowledge and Social Imagery.* London: Routledge and Keagan Paul.

Bohman, James. 1996. *Public Deliberation: Pluralism, Complexity, and Democracy.* Cambridge, MA: MIT Press.

Boisvert, Valerie and Armelle Caron. 2002. "The Convention on Biological Diversity: An Institutional Perspective of the Debates," *Journal of Economic Issues* 36(1) (March).

Bourdieu, Pierre. 1984. *Distinction: A Social Critique of the Judgment of Taste.* Cambridge, MA: Harvard University Press.

Bowd, Andrew. 2003. "The Web Rewires the Movement," *The Nation,* Aug. 4.

Bowles, Samuel and Herbert Gintis. 1976. *Schooling in Capitalist America: Educational Reform and the Contradictions of Economic Life.* New York: Basic Books.

Boyle, James. 1996. *Shamans, Software, and Spleens: Law and the Construction of the Information Society.* Cambridge, MA: Harvard University Press.

Brac de la Perriere, Robert A., et al. 2000. *Brave New Seeds: The Threat of GM Crops to Farmers.* London: Zed Books.

Brockway, Lucile H. 1988. "Plant Science and Colonial Expansion: The Botanical Chess Game." In Jack R. Kloppenburg (ed.), *Seeds and Sovereignty: The Use and Control of Plant Genetic Resources.* Durham, NC: Duke University Press.

Bromley, Hank. 1998. "How to Tell If You Really Need the Latest Technology," *Thought and Action,* Spring: 21–8.

Brown, Phil. 2000. "Popular Epidemiology and Toxic Waste Contamination: Lay and Professional Ways of Knowing." In Steve Kroll-Smith, Phil Brown, and Valerie J. Gunter (eds.), *Illness and the Environment: A Reader in Contested Medicine.* New York: NYU Press.

Brown, Phil and Edwin J. Mikkelsen. 1990. *No Safe Place: Toxic Waste, Leukemia, and Community Action.* Berkeley, CA: University of California Press.

Browne, W. P. and L. G. Hamm. 1988. "Political Choice and Social Values: The Case of bGH," *Policy Studies Journal* 17: 181–91.

Busch, Lawrence, William B. Lacy, Jeffrey Burkhardt, and Laura Lacy. 1991. *Plants, Power, and Profit: Social, Economic, and Ethical Consequences of the New Biotechnologies.* Cambridge, MA: Blackwell.

Busch, Lawrence, Keiko Tanaka, and Valerie Gunter. 2000. "Who Cares if the Rat Dies? Rodents, Risks, and Humans in the Science of Food Safety." In Steve Kroll-Smith, Phil Brown, and Valerie J. Gunter (eds.), *Illness and the Environment: A Reader in Contested Medicine.* New York: New York University Press.

Campbell, J. L. and O. K. Pedersen (eds.) 2001. *The Rise of Neoliberalism and Institutional Analysis.* Princeton: Princeton University Press.

Caro, Robert A. 1974. *The Power Broker: Robert Moses and the Fall of New York.* New York: Knopf.

Capek, Stella M. 2000. " Reframing Endometriosis: From 'Career Women's Disease' to Environment/Body Connections." In Steve Kroll-Smith, Phil Brown, and Valerie J. Gunter (eds.), *Illness and the Environment: A Reader in Contested Medicine.* New York: New York University Press.

Castellblanch, Ramon. 2000. "AIDS in Africa Drug Makers Need More Scruples," *The Toronto Star* (July 26), edition 1. Accessed via Nexis-Lexis on July 11, 2003.

Castells, Manuel. 2001. *The Internet Galaxy: Reflections on the Internet, Business, and Society.* New York: Oxford University Press.

Charles, Daniel. 2001. *Lords of the Harvest: Biotech, Big Money, and the Future of Food.* Cambridge, MA: Perseus Publishing.

Cole, Jonathan and Stephen Cole. 1973. *Social Stratification in Science.* Chicago: University of Chicago Press.

Collier, Robert. 2000. "Regulation of rbST in the US," *AgBioForum* 3(2&3): 156–63, www.agbioforum.org.

Collins, Chuck and Felice Yeskel. 2000. *Economic Apartheid in America: A Primer on Economic Inequality and Insecurity.* New York: The New Press.

Collins, Harry. 1985. *Changing Order: Replication and Induction in Scientific Practice.* Beverly Hills, CA: Sage.

Collins, Harry and Trevor Pinch. 1993. *The Golem: What Everyone Should Know About Science*. New York: Cambridge University Press.

Cordes, Colleen and Edward Miller (eds.) 2000. *Fool's Gold: A Critical Look at Computers in Childhood*. Washington, DC: Alliance for Childhood.

Crouch, Stephen R. and Steve Kroll-Smith. 2000. " Environmental Movements and Expert Knowledge: Evidence for a New Populism." In Steve Kroll-Smith, Phil Brown, and Valerie J. Gunter (eds.), *Illness and the Environment: A Reader in Contested Medicine*. New York: New York University Press.

Doble, John and Amy Richardson. 1992. "You Don't have to be a Rocket Scientist . . . ," *Technology Review*, Jan.: 51–4.

Domhoff, G. William. 1983. *Who Rules America Now? A View for the '80s*. New York: Simon and Schuster.

Dorsey, Michael K. 2001. "Shams, Shamans, and the Commercialization of Biodiversity." In Brian Tokar (ed.), *Redesigning Life? The Worldwide Challenge to Genetic Engineering*. New York: Zed Books.

Doyle, Jack. 1985. *Altered Harvest: Agriculture, Genetics and the Fate of the World's Food Supply*. New York: Viking.

Dworkin, Gerald. 1987. "Commentary: Legal and Ethical Issues," *Science, Technology, and Human Values* 12(1): 63–4.

Einsiedel, E., E. Jelsøe, & T. Breck. 2001. "Publics at the Technology Table: The Consensus Conference in Denmark, Canada, and Australia," *Public Understanding of Science* 10(1): 83–98.

Elster, Jon. 1998. "Introduction." In Jon Elster (ed.), *Deliberative Democracy*. Berkeley, CA: University of California

Epstein, Steven. 1991. "Democratic Science? AIDS Activism and the Contested Construction of Knowledge," *Socialist Review* 91: 35–64.

Epstein, Steven. 1995. "The Construction of Lay Expertise: AIDS Activism and the Forging of Credibility in the Reform of Clinical Trials," *Science, Technology, and Human Values* 20(4): 408–37.

Epstein, Steven. 1996. *Impure Science: AIDS, Activism, and the Politics of Knowledge*. Berkeley, CA: University of California Press.

Escobar, Arturo. 1997. "Cultural Politics and Biological Diversity: State, Capital, and Social Movements in the Pacific Coast of Columbia." In Orin Starn and Richard Fox (eds.), *Between Resistance and Revolution*. New Brunswick, NJ: Rutgers University Press.

ETC Group. 2002. "ETC Group Responds to Purdue University's Recent Efforts to Promote Genetic Seed Sterilization – or Terminator – as an Environmental Protection Technology," *Genotype*, May 1; www.etcgroup.org/documents/geno2002May1Purdue.pdf. Accessed Dec. 19, 2004.

Etzkowitz, Henry, Carol Kemelgor, and Brian Uzzi. 2000. *Athena Unbound: The Advancement of Women in Science and Technology*. New York: Cambridge University Press.

European Parliament. 1988a. "Hormones and the BST Hormone in the Dairy and Meat Industry." *Debates of the European Parliament* 2-367 (July 4): 11–20.

European Parliament. 1988b. "Resolution on the Effects and Risks of Using Growth Hormones and the BST Hormone in Dairy and Meat Industries (EP DOC A2-3-/88)," *Official Journal of the European Communities* C, 235/41 (July 5).

Featherman, David L. and Robert M. Hauser. 1978. *Opportunity and Change*. New York: Academic Press.

Foucault, Michel. 2002. *The Archaeology of Knowledge*. New York and London: Routledge.

Foucault, Michel. 1980. *Power/Knowledge: Selected Interviews and Other Writings*. New York: Pantheon Books.

Fox, Mary Frank. 2001. "Women, Science, and Academia: Graduate Education and Careers," *Gender and Society* 15(5): 654–66.

Fox, Mary Frank. 1995. "Women and Scientific Careers." In Sheila Jasanoff, Gerald E. Markle, James C. Petersen, and Trevor Pinch (eds.), *Handbook of Science and Technology Studies*. Thousand Oaks, CA: Sage.

Fox, Mary Frank. 2000. "Organizational Environments and Doctoral Degrees Awarded to Women in Science and Engineering Departments," *Women's Studies Quarterly* 28: 47–61.

Fox, Mary Frank. 2001. "Women, Men, and Engineering." In D. Vannoy (ed.), *Gender Mosaics: Social Perspectives*. Los Angeles, CA: Roxbury Publishing Co.

Fox, Mary Frank and Paula E. Stephan. 2001. "Careers of Young Scientists: Preferences, Prospects and Realities by Gender and Field," *Social Studies of Science* 31(1): 109–22.

Gieryn, Thomas. 1999. *Cultural Boundaries of Science: Credibility on the Line*. Chicago: University of Chicago Press.

Goodell, Rae. 1979. "Public Involvement in the DNA Controversy: The Case of Cambridge, Massachusetts," *Science, Technology, and Human Values* 27: 36–43.

Goggin, Malcolm (ed.) 1986a. *Governing Science and Technology in a Democracy*. Knoxville: University of Tennessee Press.

Goggin, Malcolm. 1986b. "Governing Science and Technology: Reconciling Science and Technology with Democracy." In M. Goggin (ed.), *Governing Science and Technology in a Democracy*. Knoxville: University of Tennessee Press.

Graham, Laurie. 1995. *On the Line at Subaru-Isuzu: The Japanese Model*. Ithaca, NY: ILR Press.

Guston, David. 1999. "Evaluating the First US Consensus Conference: The Impact of the Citizens' Panel on Telecommunications and the Future of Democracy," *Science, Technology, and Human Values* 24(4) (Oct.): 451–82.

Hacker, Sally L. 1990. *"Doing it the Hard Way": Investigations of Gender and Technology*. Boston: Unwin Hyman.

Hall, Peter. 1986. *Governing the Economy: The Politics of State Intervention in Britain and France*. Cambridge: Polity Press.

Hall, Stuart. 1982. "The Rediscovery of 'Ideology': Return of the Repressed in Media Studies." In M. Gurevitch, T. Bennett, J. Curran, and J. Woolacott (eds.), *Culture, Society and the Media*. New York: Methuen, 56–90.

Haraway, Donna. 1988. "Situated Knowledges: The Science Question in Feminism and the Privilege of Partial Perspective," *Feminist Studies* 14(3): 575–99.

Hard, Mikael and Andrew Jamison. 1998. "Conceptual Framework: Technology Debates as Appropriation Processes." In Mikael Hard and Andrew Jamison (eds.), *The Intellectual Appropriation of Technology: Discourses on Modernity, 1900–1939*. Cambridge, MA: MIT Press, 1–15.

Harding, Sandra. 1986. *The Science Question in Feminism*. Ithaca, NY: Cornell University Press.

Harrington, Jerry. 1996. "The Midwest Agricultural Chemical Association: A Regional Study of An Industry on the Defensive," *Agricultural History* 70(2): 415–38.

Haskell, Thomas. 1984. "Introduction." In Thomas Haskell (ed.), *The Authority of Expertise: Studies in History and Theory*. Bloomington: Indiana University Press.

Heller, M.A. and Rebecca S. Eisenberg. 1998. "Can Patents Deter Innovation? The Anticommons in Biomedical Research," *Science* 280 (May 1): 698–701.

Hess, David. 1997. *Science Studies: An Advanced Introduction*. New York: New York University Press.

Hilton, Isabel. 2000. "Only Westerners can Afford to be Ill," *New Statesman*, Jan. 17. Accessed via Nexis-Lexis on July 11, 2003.

Hochschild, Arlie. 1990. *The Second Shift*. New York: Avon Books.

Indyk, Debbie and David Rier. 1993. "Grassroots AIDS Knowledge: Implications for the Boundaries of Science and Collective Action," *Knowledge* 15: 3–43.

Irwin, Alan. 1995. *Citizen Science: A Study of People, Expertise, and Sustainable Development*. London: Routledge.

Jencks, Christopher, et al. 1972. *Inequality: A Reassessment of the Effect of Family and Schooling in America*. New York: Harper Colophons Books.

Jenkins, Robin. 1998. "BT in the Hot Seat," *Seedling* 15(3): 13–21.

Joerges, Bernward. 1999. "Do Politics Have Artefacts?" *Social Studies of Science* 29: 411–32.

Kahn, Joseph. 2001. "Trade Deal Near for Broad Access to Cut-Rate Drugs," *New York Times*, Nov. 13, A3.

Kanter, Rosabeth Moss. 1977. *Men and Women of the Corporation*. New York: Basic Books.

Katz, James E. and Ronald E. Rice. 2002. *Social Consequences of Internet Use: Access, Involvement, and Interaction*. Cambridge, MA: MIT Press.

Kenney, Martin and Richard Florida. 1993. *Beyond Mass Production: The Japanese System and its Transfer to the U.S.* New York: Oxford University Press.

Kleinman, Daniel Lee. 1986. "Biotechnology for Sale: Monsanto and the Bio-technology Controversy," *Wisconsin Academy Review* 33: 23–6.

Kleinman, Daniel Lee. 1995: *Politics on the Endless Frontier: Postwar Research Policy in the United States*. Durham, NC: Duke University Press.

Kleinman, Daniel Lee. 2003. *Impure Cultures: University Biology and the World of Commerce*. Madison, WI: University of Wisconsin Press.

Kleinman, Daniel Lee and Abby J. Kinchy. 2003a. "Boundaries in Science Policy-making: Bovine Growth Hormone in the European Union," *Sociological Quarterly* 44(4): 577–95.

Kleinman, Daniel Lee and Abby J. Kinchy. 2003b. "Why Ban Bovine Growth Hormone?: Science, Social Welfare, and the Divergent Biotech Policy Landscapes in Europe and the United States," *Science as Culture* 12(3): 375–414.

Kleinman, Daniel Lee and Jack Kloppenburg, Jr. 1991. "Aiming for the Discursive High Ground: Monsanto and the Biotechnology Controversy," *Sociological Forum* 6(3): 427–47.

Kleinman, Daniel Lee and Susan Pastor. 1989. "BGH Root Issue Socioeconomic Impact on the Small Family Farm," *The Capital Times* (Madison, WI), Sept. 7.

Kleinman, Daniel Lee and Steven P. Vallas. 2001. "Science, Capitalism, and the Rise of the 'Knowledge Worker: The Changing Structure of Knowledge Production in the United States," *Theory and Society* 30: 451–92.

Kleinman, Daniel Lee and Steven P. Vallas. Forthcoming. "Contradiction in Convergence: University and Industry in the Biotechnology Field." In Scott Frickel and Kelly Moore (eds.), *The New Political Sociology of Science: Institutions, Networks, and Power*. Madison, WI: University of Wisconsin Press.

Kloppenburg, Jack R. 1988. *First the Seed: The Political Economy of Biotechnology, 1492–2000*. New York: Cambridge University Press.

Kloppenburg, Jack, Jr. 2000. "Biopiracy, Witchery, and the Fables of Ecoliberalism," *Peace Review* 12(4): 509–16.

Kloppenburg, Jack R. 2004. *First the Seed: The Political Economy of Biotechnology, 1492–2000*. Second edition. Madison, WI: University of Wisconsin Press.

Kloppenburg, Jack R. and Martin Kenney. 1984. "Biotechnology, Seeds, and the Restructuring of Agriculture," *Insurgent Sociologist* 12 (Fall): 3–17.

Kloppenburg, Jack R. and Daniel Lee Kleinman. 1987. "Seed Wars: Common Heritage, Private Property, and Political Strategy," *Socialist Review* 95: 7–41.

Kloppenburg, Jack and Daniel Lee Kleinman. 1988. "Plant Genetic Resources, the Common Bowl." In Jack R. Kloppenburg (ed.), *Seeds and Sovereignty: The Use and Control of Plant Genetic Resources*. Durham, NC: Duke University Press.

Kohn, Gustave. 1987. "Agriculture, Pesticides, and the American Chemical Industry." In Gino Marco, Robert Hollingsworth, and William Durham (eds.), *Silent Spring Revisited*. Washington, DC: American Chemical Society.

Kozol, Jonathan. 1991. *Savage Inequalities: Children in America's Schools*. New York: Harper Perennial.

Krimsky, Sheldon. 1982. *Genetic Alchemy: The Social History of the Recombinant DNA Controversy*. Cambridge, MA: MIT Press.

Krimsky, Sheldon. 1984a. "Epistemic Considerations on the Value of Folk-Wisdom in Science and Technology," *Policy Studies Review* 3(2): 246–62.

Krimsky, Sheldon. 1984b. "Beyond Technocracy: New Routes for Citizen Involvement in Social Risk Assessment. " In J. Petersen (ed.), *Citizen Participation in Science Policy*. Amherst: University of Massachusetts Press, 43–61.

Krimsky, Sheldon. 1986a. "Research Under Community Standards: Three Case Studies," *Science, Technology, and Human Values* 11: 14–33.

Krimsky, Sheldon. 1986b. "Local Control of Research Involving Chemical Warfare Agents." In M. Goggin (ed.), *Governing Science and Technology in a Democracy*. Knoxville: University of Tennessee Press.

Krimsky, Sheldon and Roger Wrubel. 1996. *Agricultural Biotechnology and the Environment: Science, Policy, and Social Issues*. Urbana, IL: University of Illinois Press.

Kuhn, Thomas S. 1970. *The Structure of Scientific Revolutions*. Second edition. Chicago: Chicago University Press.

Lacey, Hugh. 2003. "Seeds and their Sociocultural Nexus." In Robert Figueroa and Sandra Harding (eds.), *Science and Other Cultures: Issues in Philosophies of Science and Technology*. New York: Routledge.

Lacy, William. 2000. "Agricultural Biotechnology Policy, Socioeconomic Issues, and the Fourth Criterion." In *Encyclopedia of Ethical, Legal and Policy Issues in Biotechnology*. New York: John Wiley and Sons.

Laird, Frank. 1993. "Participatory Analysis, Democracy, and Technological Decision Making," *Science, Technology, and Human Values* 18(3): 341–61.

Lambrecht, B. 1999. "Amazon Tribal Leaders Challenge U.S. Patent," *St. Louis Post-Dispatch*, March 31.

Latour, Bruno. 1987. *Science in Action: How to Follow Scientists and Engineers Through Society*. Cambridge, MA: Harvard University Press.

Levitt, Norman and Paul Gross. 1994. "The Perils of Democratizing Science," *The Chronicle of Higher Education*, Oct. 5, B1, B2.

Lessig, Lawrence. 2001. *The Future of Ideas: The Fate of the Commons in a Connected World*. New York: Random House.

Lilliston, Ben. 2001. "Farmers Fight to Save Organic Crops," *The Progressive*, Sept.

Lohr, Steve. 2002. "Digital (Fill in the Blank) is on the Horizon," *New York Times*, Aug. 1, A1, C4

Lorber, Judith. 1994. *Paradoxes of Gender*. New Haven: Yale University Press.

Lowi, Theodore J. 1967. "Party, Policy, and Constitution in America." In William Nisbet Chambers and Walter Dean Burnham (eds.), *The American Party System*. New York: Oxford University Press.

Lukes, Steven. 1974. *Power: A Radical View*. London: Macmillan.

MacKinnon, Catharine A. 1989. *Toward a Feminist Theory of the State*. Cambridge, MA: Harvard University Press.

MacLeod, Jay. 1995. *Ain't No Makin' It: Aspirations and Attainment in a Low-Income Neighborhood*. Second edition. Boulder, CO: Westview Press.

Martin, Brian. 2005. "Agricultural Antibiotics: Features of a Controversy." In Daniel Lee Kleinman, Abby J. Kinchy, and Jo Handelsman (eds.), *Controversies in Science and Technology, Volume 1: From Maize to Menopause*. Madison, WI: University of Wisconsin Press.

Martin, Emily. 1991. "The Egg and the Sperm: How Science has Constructed a Romance Based on Stereotypical Male–Female Roles," *Signs* 16: 485–501.

Marx, Karl. 1977. *Karl Marx: Selected Writings*, ed. David McLellan. New York: Oxford University Press.

McCourt, Tom and Patrick Burkhart. 2003. "When Creators, Corporations, and Consumers Collide: Napster and the Development of On-Line Music Distribution," *Media, Culture, and Society* 25: 333–50.

McIlwee, Judith S. and J. Gregg Robinson. 1992. *Women in Engineering: Gender, Power, and Workplace Culture*. Albany, NY: State University of New York Press.

McNeil, Donald G., Jr. 2001. "Patents or Poverty? New Debate over Lack of AIDS Care in Africa," *New York Times*, Nov. 5, A6.

Merson, John. 2001. "Bio-prospecting or Bio-piracy: Intellectual Property Rights and Biodiversity in a Colonial and Postcolonial Context," *Osiris*, 282–96.

Merton, Robert K. 1973. *The Sociology of Science: Theoretical and Empirical Investigations*. Chicago: University of Chicago Press.

Meyer, John W. and Brian Rowan. 1977. "Institutionalized Organizations: Formal Structure as Myth and Ceremony,' *American Journal of Sociology* 83: 340–63.

Mitroff, I. I. 1974. "Norms and Counternorms in a Select Group of Appollo Moon Scientists: A Case Study of the Ambivalence of Scientists," *American Sociological Review* 39: 579–95.

Mooney, Patrick Roy. 1983. "The Law of the Seed," *Development Dialogue* 1–2: 1–72.

Monsanto. 1999. "Global Harvest: Biotechnology and Imported Food." St. Louis: Monsanto Corporation.

Moran, Katy, Steven R. King, and Thomas J. Carlson. 2001. " Biodiversity Prospecting: Lessons and Prospects," *Annual Review of Anthropology* 30: 505–26.

Mulkay, Michael. 1980. "Interpretation and the Use of Rules: The Case of Norms in Science." In Thomas Gieryn (ed.), *Science and Social Structure: A Festschrift for Robert K. Merton*. New York: New York Academy of Science.

Murmann, Johann P. and Ralph Landau. 1998. "On the Making of Competitive Advantage: The Development of the Chemical Industries in Britain and German Since 1850." In A. Arora, R. Landau, and N. Rosenberg (eds.), *Chemicals and Long-Term Economic Growth: Insights from the Chemical Industry*. New York: John Wiley and Sons, Inc.

Nelkin, Dorothy. 1995. "Scientific Controversies: The Dynamics of Public Disputes in the United States." In S. Jasanoff, G. E. Markle, J. C. Petersen, and T. Pinch (eds.), *Handbook of Science and Technology Studies*. Thousand Oaks, CA: Sage Publications, 444–56.

Nelkin, Dorothy. 1984. "Science and Technology Policy and the Democratic Process." In James Petersen (ed.), *Citizen Participation in Science Policy*. Amherst: University of Massachusetts Press, 18–39.

Noble, David. 2001. *Digital Diploma Mills: The Automation of Higher Education*. New York: Monthly Review Press.

Noble, David. 1984. *Forces of Production: A Social History of Industrial Automation*. New York: Knopf.

Noble, David. 1983. "Present Tense Technology: Part One," *Democracy* 3: 8–24.

Norris, Pippa. 2001. *Digital Divide: Civic Engagement, Information Poverty, and the Internet Worldwide*. New York: Cambridge University Press.

OMB Watch. 2003. "Income Watch: The Rich are Getting Richer and Getting Bigger Tax Breaks," *OMB Watch* 4(13): June 30.

Office of Technology Assessment, US Congress. 1991. *U.S. Dairy Industry at a Crossroad: Biotechnology and Policy Choices: Special Report*. OTA-F-470. Washington, DC: Superintendent of Documents, US Government Printing Office, May.

Owen-Smith, Jason. 2001. "Managing Laboratory Work through Skepticism: Processes of Evaluation and Control," *American Sociological Review* 66 (June): 427–52.

Palladino, Paulo. 1996. *Entomology, Ecology, and Agriculture: The Making of Scientific Careers in North America*. Amsterdam: Harwood Academic Publishers.

Perkins, John H. 1982. *Insects, Experts, and the Insecticide Crisis: The Quest for New Pest Management Strategies*. New York: Plenium.

Pesticide Action Network. 1999. "New Patents for Terminator Seeds Threaten Farmers and Food Security." Press Release, Feb. 1.

Philip, Kavita. 2001. " Seeds of Neo-Colonialism? Reflections on Ecological Politics in the New World Order," *Capitalism, Nature, Socialism* 12(2) (June): 3–47.

Pollack, Andrew. 2001. "Clash Over Patents," *New York Times*, April 20, A6.

Pomerleau, Andrée, Daniel Bolduc, Gérard Malcuit, and Louise Cossette. 1990. "Pink or Blue: Environmental Gender Stereotypes in the First Two Years of Life," *Sex Roles: A Journal of Research* 22: 359–67.

Posey, Darell A. and Graham Dutfield. 1996. *Beyond Intellectual Property: Toward Traditional Resource Rights for Indigenous Peoples and Local Communities.* Ottawa, Canada: International Development Research Centre.

Proctor, Robert. 1991. *Value Free Science?: Purity and Power in Modern Knowledge.* Cambridge, MA: Harvard University Press

Robinson, J. Gregg and Judith S. McIlwee. 1989. " Women in Engineering: A Promise Unfulfilled?" *Social Problems* 36(5): 455–72.

Rural Advancement Fund International. 1997. *Human Nature: Agricultural Biodiversity and Farm-Based Food Security.* Ottawa, Canada: Rural Advancement Fund International.

Sadker, Myra and David Sadker. 1994. *Failing at Fairness: How Our Schools Cheat Girls.* New York: Touchstone.

Samuelson, Pamela. 1987. "Innovation and Competition: Conflicts over Intellectual Property in New Technology," *Science, Technology, and Human Values* 11(1): 6–21.

Sawyer, Richard. C. 1996. *To Make a Spotless Orange: Biological Control in California.* Ames, IA: Iowa State University Press.

Saxenian, Annalee. 1994. *Regional Advantage: Culture and Competition in Silicon Valley and Route 128.* Cambridge, MA: Harvard University Press.

Schatzberg, Eric. 1999. *Wings of Wood, Wings of Metal: Culture and Technical Choice in American Airplane Materials, 1914–1945.* Princeton, NJ: Princeton University Press.

Sclove, Richard. 1995. *Democracy and Technology.* New York: The Guilford Press.

Seashore, Karen, David Blumenthal, Michael Gluck, and Michael Soto. 1989. "Entrepreneurs in Academe: An Exploration of Behavior Among Life Scientists," *Administrative Science Quarterly* 34: 110–31.

Servon, Lisa J. 2002. *Bridging the Digital Divide: Technology, Community, and Public Policy.* Malden, MA: Blackwell Publishing.

Shadid, Anthony. 2001. "Gentic Drift Affects More than Biology – US Farmers Stand to Lose Millions," *Boston Globe*, April 8.

Shapin, Steven. 1994. *A Social History of Truth: Civility and Science in Seventeenth-Century England.* Chicago: University of Chicago Press.

Shefter, Martin. 1977. "Party and Patronage: Germany, England, and Italy," *Politics and Society* 7(4): 403–52.

Shiva, Vandana. 1997. *Biopiracy: The Plunder of Nature and Knowledge.* Boston: South End Press.

Shulman, Seth. 1999. *Owning the Future.* Boston: Houghton Mifflin.

Simon, Stephanie. 2001. "Biotech Soybeans Plant Seed of Risky Revolution," *Los Angeles Times*, July 1, A1, 18, 19.

Sismondo, Sergio. 2004. *An Introduction to Science and Technology Studies.* Malden, MA: Blackwell Publishing.

Skocpol, Theda. 1985. "Bringing the State Back In: Strategies of Analysis in Current Research." In Peter B. Evans, Dietrich Rueschemeyer, and Theda Skocpol, *Bringing the State Back In.* New York: Cambridge University Press.

Smith, Merritt Roe. 1995. "Technological Determinism in American Culture." In Merritt Roe Smith and Leo Marx (eds.), *Does Technology Drive History: The Dilemma of Technological Determinism.* Cambridge, MA: MIT Press.

Smith-Doerr, Laurel. 2004. "Flexibility and Fairness: Effects of the Network Form of Organization on Gender Equity in Life Science Careers," *Sociological Perspectives* 47(1) (Spring): 25–54.

Sophia, Zoe. 1998. "The Mythic Machine: Gendered Irrationalities and Computer Culture." In Hank Bromley and Michael W. Apple (eds.), *Education/ Technology/Power: Educational Computing as Social Practice.* Albany, NY: State University of New York Press.

Spanier, Bonnie. 1995. *Im/Partial Science: Gender Ideology in Molecular Biology.* Bloomington, IN: Indiana University Press.

Sperber, Irwin. 1990. *Fashions in Science: Opinion Leaders and Collective Behavior in the Social Sciences.* Minneapolis, MN: University of Minnesota Press.

Stein, Jason. 2002. "Controversy in a Sweet Discovery," *Wisconsin State Journal* (Nov. 5): A1, A9.

Stokes, Donald E. 1997. *Pasteur's Quadrant: Basic Science and Technological Innovation.* Washington, DC: Brookings Institution Press.

Sunstein, Cass. 2001. *Republic.com.* Princeton, NJ: Princeton University Press.

Swarns, Rachel L. 2001. "Drug Makers Drop Suit over AIDS Medicine," *New York Times*, April 20, A1, A6.

US Department of Commerce, National Telecommunications and Information Administration. 1995. *Falling Through the Net: A Survey of the 'Have Nots' in Rural and Urban America.* Washington, DC: National Telecommunications and Information Administration.

US Department of Commerce, National Telecommunications and Information Administration. 1999. *Falling Through the Net: Defining the Digital Divide. A Report on the Telecommunications and Information Technology Gap in America.* Washington, DC: National Telecommunications and Information Administration.

US Department of Commerce, National Telecommunications and Information Administration. 2000. *Falling Through the Net: Toward Digital Inclusion. A Report on Americans' Access to Technology Tools.* Washington, DC: National Telecommunications and Information Administration.

US House of Representatives. 1983. *Hearing Before the Subcommittee on Investigations and Oversight and the Subcommittee on Science, Research and Technology of the Committee on Science and Technology,* 98th Congress, 1st Session, June22. Washington, DC: US Government Printing Office.

US House of Representatives. 1986. "Review of Status and Potential Impact of Bovine Growth Hormone," *Hearing before the Subcommittee on Livestock, Dairy, and Poultry of the Committee on Agriculture,* 99th Congress, Second Session, June 11. Washington DC: US Government Printing Office.

US Senate. 1975. *Hearing before the Subcommittee on Health of the Committee on Labor and Public Welfare*, 94th Congress, 1st Session, April 22nd. Washington, DC: US Government Printing Office.

Vaidhyanathan, Siva. 2001. *Copyrights and Copywrongs: The Rise of Intellectual Property and How it Threatens Creativity.* New York: NYU Press.

Warschauer, Mark. 2003. *Technology and Social Inclusion: Rethinking the Digital Divide.* Cambridge, MA: MIT Press.

Weber, Max. 1978. *Economy and Society*, vol. 2, eds. Guenther Roth and Claus Wittich. Berkeley, CA: University of California Press.

Weber, Rachel N. 1999. "Manufacturing Gender in Military Cockpit Design." In Donald MacKenzie and Judy Wajcman (eds.), *The Social Shaping of Technology.* Second edition. Buckingham, UK: Open University Press.

Wing, Steve. 2000. "Limits of Epidemiology." In Steve Kroll-Smith, Phil Brown, and Valerie J. Gunter (eds.), *Illness and the Environment: A Reader in Contested Medicine.* New York: New York University Press.

Winner, Langdon. 1986. *The Whale and the Reactor.* Chicago: University of Chicago Press.

Woodforde, John. 1970. *The Story of the Bicycle.* London: Routledge and Kegan Paul.

Wynne, Brian. 1992. "Misunderstood Misunderstanding: Social Identities and Public Uptake of Science," *Public Understanding of Science* 1: 281–304.

Wynne, Brian. 1996. "May the Sheep Safely Graze? A Reflexive View of the Expert-lay Knowledge Divide." In S. Lash, B. Szerszynski, and B. Wynne (eds.), *Risk, Environment and Modernity: Towards a New Ecology.* London: Sage Publications.

Xie, Yu and Kimberlee A. Shauman. 2003. *Women in Science: Career Processes and Outcomes.* Cambridge, MA: Harvard University Press.

Yearly, Steven. 2000. "What Does Science Mean in the 'Public Understanding of Science'?" In Meinolf Dierkes and Claudia von Grote (eds.), *Between Understanding and Trust: The Public, Science, and Technology.* Amsterdam: Harwood Academic Publishers.

Index